Changing
How the World
Does Business

Changing How the World Does Business

*FedEx's Incredible Journey
to Success—The Inside Story*

ROGER FROCK

BK

BERRETT-KOEHLER PUBLISHERS, INC.
San Francisco

Berrett-Koehler Publishers, Inc.
235 Montgomery Street, Suite 650
San Francisco, CA 94104-2916
Tel: (415) 288-0260   Fax: (415) 362-2512   www.bkconnection.com

Ordering Information

Quantity sales. Special discounts are available on quantity purchases by corporations, associations, and others. For details, contact the "Special Sales Department" at the Berrett-Koehler address above.

Individual sales. Berrett-Koehler publications are available through most bookstores. They can also be ordered directly from Berrett-Koehler: Tel: (800) 929-2929; Fax: (802) 864-7626; www.bkconnection.com

Orders for college textbook/course adoption use. Please contact Berrett-Koehler: Tel: (800) 929-2929; Fax: (802) 864-7626.

Orders by U.S. trade bookstores and wholesalers. Please contact Publishers Group West, 1700 Fourth Street, Berkeley, CA 94710. Tel: (510) 528-1444; Fax (510) 528-3444.

Production Management: Michael Bass Associates

Berrett-Koehler and the BK logo are registered trademarks of Berrett-Koehler Publishers, Inc.

Printed in the United States of America

Berrett-Koehler books are printed on long-lasting acid-free paper. When it is available, we choose paper that has been manufactured by environmentally responsible processes. These may include using trees grown in sustainable forests, incorporating recycled paper, minimizing chlorine in bleaching, or recycling the energy produced at the paper mill.

Library of Congress Cataloging-in-Publication Data
  Frock, Roger, 1936–
    Changing how the world does business : FedEx's incredible journey to success : the inside story / by Roger Frock.
      p. cm.
    Includes bibliographical references and index.
    ISBN-10: 1-57675-413-8; ISBN-13: 978-1-57675-413-9 (hardcover : alk. paper)
    1. Federal Express Corporation—History. 2. Express service—United States—History. I. Title.
    HE5903.F435F73 2006
    388'.044—dc22
                                          2006009520

First Edition
11 10 09 08 07 06   10 9 8 7 6 5 4 3 2 1

To my lovely wife, Linda,
who has provided encouragement throughout this
endeavor and taught me the true meaning of love

Contents

Foreword

When Roger Frock called to tell me he was writing a book about the early days of Federal Express, I felt that finally the right man had stepped forward to chronicle this dramatic bit of business history. From late 1973 to the spring of 1978, as head of the board of directors' executive committee, I participated in most aspects of the company's business during the startup. In those early years, Federal Express hovered on the verge of bankruptcy. Murphy's Law, "Anything that can go wrong will go wrong," certainly applied. Finally, a strong, growing, and profitable business emerged and we turned the corner. As one of my partners retrospectively exclaimed, it was like taking a supertanker at full speed over a reef with a quarter inch to spare!

There was a lot more at stake in the future of Federal Express than the fortunes of its management and shareholders. Federal Express was a major endeavor of a fledgling venture capital industry to create something new in a very public arena. Venture capital was a relatively unknown business at the time, and as far as the public knew, if a project succeeded, a few rich guys got richer; if there was failure, no one ever really heard about it. But with Federal Express, some venture capitalists were doing more than just writing checks. They were very publicly getting their hands dirty in a day-to-day survival operation. If matters had gone in the wrong direction, I am sure the venture capital business would be different than it is today.

Roger and the other people associated with the company worked full-time, essentially 24/7. I was a part-timer who flew in once a month, sometimes more frequently, to deal with financial issues and policy matters. I have never worked with a more dedicated group of people. All were intelligent, hardworking, able people with a high regard for one another. They were flexible, worked together as a unified team, quickly adapted to new challenges, and never got discouraged, no matter what kind of hot water the company was in.

In early 1973 I was an executive vice president of New Court Securities Corporation, a New York–based private investment affiliate of various Rothschild banking interests. My principal responsibilities were to manage the venture capital assets of the firm. At the time, we had about $75 million under our care, which made us one of the largest pools of venture capital in the United States. The investment climate was not good. Stocks had been in decline for several years, and many middle-market companies with good earnings and decent balance sheets were selling for six or seven times earnings. Moreover, inflation had reared its ugly head, interest rates were rising, and money was getting tight. There were no initial public offerings in sight, nor had there been for several years. For the time being, the day of the small venture deal with its long-time horizon to liquidity was over.

At New Court, we were obliged to modify our investment strategy to suit the changing capital markets. Typically, we would invest in small or startup companies and look toward living with them for a period of years while they realized their business plan. Sometimes we might step in financially when other sources of capital such as banks or other investors became unavailable. From what we could see in early 1973, there was going to be a financial drought for smaller enterprise for some period ahead. Consequently, we began to focus on those investment opportunities that could achieve financial critical mass fairly promptly. An investment opportunity that could reach $100 million in revenues and commensurate high margins and cash flow in a few years had a chance. It was our view that the IPO market would come back but new ventures would have to demonstrate something remarkable to attract the institutional investor.

One day George Montgomery of White, Weld & Company called to ask us to look over an intriguing situation they had uncovered in Memphis. He described a 28-year-old, ex-marine captain, a Vietnam veteran with a Silver Star, a Yale graduate, who had started with his own money a small-package airline with great potential.

Fred Smith turned out to be a very attractive person, highly articulate and obviously very intelligent. He had studied the small-package delivery business inside and out, and he had developed some very innovative ideas as to how to serve it. He also had a very competent management group working night and day to turn this operation into reality. In short, this was not a scheme on paper but one in three dimensions into which he had poured a good part of his net worth. Fred was about as entrepreneurial as they come.

In the early morning hours of April 20, 1973, a group of individuals—Fred Smith, Roger Frock, and I—stood watch outside the old World War II hangars at the Memphis airport for the first full run of the Federal Express Falcon 20 fleet. In due course, these aircraft came roaring out of the night sky. During the next several hours, they were unloaded and reloaded, and took off just before dawn. It was an impressive sight that reminded me of an old war movie, *Twelve O'clock High*.

Next morning we sat through a presentation presided over by Roger Frock. Needless to say, I was frazzled by travel time and lack of sleep. Roger, on the other hand, who had not made it to bed, was fresh, put together, and ready to go. He was the general manager and chief of operations, and I gathered he was no stranger to all-nighters. He was not a hip shooter; his convictions stemmed from hard study and a pragmatic turn of mind.

Back in New York, we began to focus on all the information and evidence we had to support a significant investment in Federal Express. First, we concluded the terms offered were inadequate to support the inherent risk and the level of support required to make the venture work. Second, the time limits to a decision were very tight—Federal Express had no time cushion before it had to exercise its options on the Falcon aircraft it had under contract.

Furthermore, we were not certain this new enterprise could generate a positive cash flow quickly enough to support the large capital investment and big debt structure that was contemplated. Most important, there was no operating record on which to hang one's hat, and no clear-cut evidence that the system could generate profits. Like all investment decisions, this one offered a great many positives but some profound negatives as well. Reluctantly, New Court decided not to participate. New Court took itself out of the running because we could not see ourselves solving all the problems we had uncovered. The time requirements to do all the studies or due diligence to support the figures and meet the fleet option deadlines were just too tight.

We later re-examined our thinking about Federal Express after another potential investor, General Dynamics, turned out a favorable report. Now we had General Dynamics' very comprehensive study to support our own thinking, as well as the potential participation of other serious investors who could help provide the resources needed to get this job done. We decided to join forces with White, Weld to assist it in getting this difficult financing completed. We also became the lead investor in the transaction. When I asked my partners who would represent us in this affair, they all turned toward me and smiled. It wasn't going to be easy.

Our faith and hard work began to pay off by 1975, as Federal's small-package business began to tax the capacity of its airplanes. Major cities in the Northeast along with Chicago, Los Angeles, and San Francisco were requiring two or more flights a day to meet growing demand. Suddenly, new vistas of what Federal Express could become opened up. There was the strong possibility that the company would become much larger and more profitable than any of us had thought possible, and we could finally look forward to a public offering.

The successful initial public offering of Federal Express in April of 1978 ended the long drought in new issues and was a bellwether of good things to follow. The tide had turned and a lot of other boats were to be lifted. Federal's shareholders were well rewarded, and for the next five years, the company grew at an astonishing rate both in sales and in earnings.

In the late eighties and early nineties the company faltered as it absorbed significant losses from ZapMail, the acquisition of Flying Tigers Airline, and its poorly conceived assault on the small-package market of Western Europe. The U.S. domestic package business absorbed all of these losses, however, and the company remained intact. Fred Smith and his management team had finally organized the template for a truly remarkable $30 billion company called FedEx.

This book chronicles the dramatic last-minute saves and turn-arounds the company engineered from its inception to the present. It will introduce you to the remarkable individuals who gave Fred's initial concept wings and whose flexibility and creativity made a fledgling startup into one of the great success stories in modern business.

Charles Lewis Lea, Jr.
Director of Federal Express, 1973–1978

Acknowledgments

first wish to express my thanks to my wonderful wife, Linda, who, while writing her own book, has encouraged me, served as my coach, offered recollections from her own work experiences at Federal Express, and supported my efforts throughout this process.

Special thanks go to those who gave so willingly of their time to share their personal recollections and insights during the interviews, including Michael Basch, Charles Brandon, Nathaniel Breed, Michael Fitzgerald, Joseph Hinson, Charles Lewis Lea, John Tucker Morse, Debra Mouton, Dennis Sweeney, Leon Tyree, Theodore Weise, and Peter Willmott. Thanks also to those who are so much a part of this story and who, except for their untimely deaths, would have contributed their personal remembrances: Arthur Bass, John Vincent Fagan, and James Riedmeyer.

I also express my appreciation to Justine and Michael Toms of New Dimensions World Broadcasting Network, who saw merit in my early work, and Steve Piersanti of Berrett-Koehler Publishers, who made instrumental suggestions throughout the early editorial process. I want to acknowledge the tremendous contributions made by my content editor, Valerie Andrews, who guided me through the process of turning rambling recollections into prose worthy of this incredible story.

Finally, I want to thank Kathy Oddenino, whose inspired teachings have reminded me of the importance of "knowing thyself," the many friends and associates who have encouraged me to write this book, and Fred Smith for making it possible.

Introduction

A Case History of
Courage and Tenacity

FedEx has changed the way we do business, allowing established firms to expand their services throughout the world and helping smaller companies to look and act like corporate giants, making overnight connections with global markets. Its founders helped to restructure the transportation industry and created a unique corporate culture that has placed FedEx among the most successful new ventures of the past 50 years.

Fortune magazine has described FedEx as one of the top ten business triumphs of the 1970s and lists the firm as one of the Top 10 Most Admired Companies in America and the world; one of 100 Best Companies to Work For in America, among which it has been listed continuously since 1998; and one of the 50 Best Companies for Minorities.

The company has also received similar accolades and recognition from the *Wall Street Journal, Business Week, Computerworld, Wired, Logistics Management and Distribution, Information Week, Business Ethics, Forbes, Air Cargo World*, and *Financial Times*. Internationally, FedEx has been recognized as one of the best employers in Canada, Switzerland, Brazil, Latin America, Mexico, Chile, Hong Kong, Singapore, Korea, the Philippines, India, and Argentina.

In its original incarnation as Federal Express, the firm developed a completely new concept of customer service, pioneered technical advances for the entire transportation industry, and significantly altered our work

1

environment. People can now live and work outside major metropolitan cities by utilizing FedEx's exceptional reach and reliability to connect with other areas of the business world. We can now move radiopharmaceuticals with short shelf lives and critical blood samples overnight and ship products directly from manufacturer to consumer, greatly simplifying the distribution chain.

While FedEx is now a household word, the company that invented overnight delivery was far from an overnight success. The inside story is one of great interest to anyone starting a new business, for it highlights the extraordinary combination of grit and determination, teamwork and creative thinking, luck and perseverance needed to keep a company afloat in its early stages.

I had the good fortune to be a member of the initial team assembled by Fred Smith, the founder of Federal Express. We experienced difficulties and near disasters, but we also had our share of good fortune and occasional help from some surprising sources. On several occasions, we came within an inch of failure, because of dwindling financial resources, regulatory roadblocks, or unforeseen events like the Arab oil embargo. Once, Fred's luck at the gaming tables of Las Vegas helped to save the company from financial disaster. Another time, we had to ask our employees to hold their paychecks while we waited for the next wave of financing.

Fred's tenacious drive and brilliant leadership got us through crisis after crisis. However, no individual can create and build a successful enterprise without the help of others. This book contains the personal insights of the people who took part in the FedEx startup—many appear for the first time in print. This is the insider's view, full of cliffhangers and last-minute saves that show the trials faced by anyone launching a new business.

The FedEx story shows the careful planning required for a startup and the flexibility and quick thinking needed to deal with unanticipated challenges. Knowledgeable professionals evaluated the Federal Express concept, researched the potential market for the service, investigated the competition, and prepared a startup plan. However, the concept went through several critical adjustments on its roller-coaster ride to success. In this book, I set out to explore the process of innovation and the character traits needed to move a promising vision into the real world.

FedEx went through several periods of risk and turmoil, yet breakthroughs often followed our periods of deep apprehension and doubt. Our final lesson is a positive one: If the concept is right, courage and tenacity can tilt the odds in one's favor.

The FedEx story is also an antidote to the negative press big business has received in the past few years. We read every day about the greed, the lies, and the fraudulent practices in both the private and public sector. The founders of FedEx were not perfect, but their basic operating principles of integrity, truth, equality, and personal responsibility provide a model for others to emulate. In a rapidly changing business climate, we valued open communications and cooperation at every level of the organization. FedEx created a win-win climate for all of its constituents, providing security for its employees, reliable service for its customers, and a fair return to its shareholders.

After the Enron and WorldCom scandals, the Securities and Exchange Commission issued its requirement that chief executive officers attest to the correctness of their financial reports. FedEx was one of the first major corporations to do so, without requesting extra time for review, because its CEO had created an ethical climate and remained closely involved with the company's day-to-day operations.

It is my fondest hope that this book will serve as a principled guide for new startups as well as established companies, and perhaps even convince a few of the ethically challenged to reexamine their options. It *is* possible for an organization to operate with ethical principles and still be successful.

The front-row seat to FedEx's incredible journey to success that this book offers will appeal to a wide and diverse audience. In addition to those launching new enterprises, business analysts will profit from this firsthand account of the company's growth from startup to maturity. Executives desiring to improve their leadership skills can learn from the strategy and tactics employed by Fred Smith and his leadership team. Finally, managers and supervisors can learn how to motivate employees and encourage innovative thinking.

For convenience, the book is organized chronologically.

- PART I examines the development of the concept, with the initial goal of transporting small time-sensitive packages overnight, and the initial feasibility studies.

- PART II describes the operating plans, initial management staff, regulatory roadblocks, and inauguration of the service.

- PART III focuses on the company's continuing financial struggles and expansion of the service network.

- PART IV recounts the growth of the organization up to the first public offering.

- PART V explores the transformation from a startup company to a mature organization and shows the growing pains that FedEx endured.

- PART VI looks at the corporate culture that is largely responsible for the company's success and how FedEx has changed the way others do business.

FedEx today has annual revenues of $30 billion, more than 250,000 employees, and a fleet of over six hundred aircraft; operates more than 70,000 surface vehicles; and provides service to over two hundred countries, representing most of the industrial world. On a typical day, the company handles nearly six million important time-critical packages and larger freight shipments. It is, in fact, one of the largest transportation companies in the world, ranking in the top five in revenue among the world's airlines.

The rise of this company rests on two key innovations. The first is the hub-and-spokes network—the system used to move packages and documents from origin to destination. The hub, located in Memphis, Tennessee, is the facility for sorting packages and documents. The spokes of the network are the routes to and from the originating cities. Packages picked up from shippers in the afternoon are flown to the hub before midnight, sorted to outbound flights within two hours, and delivered to their destination the following morning. No one had ever created such a simple and elegant process to move time-sensitive packages from place to place.

However, our employees and unique supporting culture were equally important contributors to the success of the company. At several places, I refer to the "purple blood" attitude of the FedEx employees, borrowing a color from our logo to describe the impassioned workers who were the lifeblood of our company. I have included stories about the dedication and contributions of these remarkable individuals who stood by us from the beginning, when outsiders ridiculed our efforts and called our vision crazy. As Tom Morris observes in *If Aristotle Ran General Motors,* "it is the people within any enterprise and their interactions that ultimately produce excellence or mediocrity."

Building Federal Express from concept to triumph was a wonderfully rewarding business adventure. Fred Smith's beginning concept and dynamic leadership inspired us all, but it took an incomparable workforce to turn his vision into reality. I am fortunate to have been a part of FedEx's incredible journey and honored to be the one putting our tale into print.

PART I

From Skepticism to Affirmation
Before May 1972

The Trail of Inspiration

edEx originated the modern integrated priority package express industry, the first small-package airline to maintain direct control of shipments with a self-contained transportation system from pickup to delivery. Millions of people rely on FedEx every day for their most important business and personal deliveries whenever and wherever they must have overnight and time-definite service. The delivery service is so much a part of our lives that we can barely recall living without it.

It seems that FedEx has always been there, ready to respond to our most urgent needs, yet few people know how it was first conceived. When its efficient hub-and-spokes network was originally proposed, the concept was ridiculed as impractical. Existing regulations prohibited this form of nationwide delivery service, experts considered it a financial impossibility, and airline executives forecast its demise.

To understand the mountainous road to success, we must look back more than 40 years to glimpse the early dreams that inspired and motivated Frederick Wallace Smith, the Mississippi-born founder of the company.

THE YALE PAPER

Legend has it that the inspiration for Federal Express came from a paper Fred hurriedly wrote in the mid-1960s near the end of his sophomore year at Yale University. Fred was an avid reader with an interest in a wide variety of subjects, a student of military and aviation history, and a creative and imaginative thinker. Already an accomplished flyer with a keen interest in aviation, Fred had reestablished the Yale Flying Club, first organized in the 1930s by Juan Trippe, the founder of Pan American World Airways.

Fred recalls submitting a term paper that pointed out problems associated with moving airfreight on passenger planes, concluding that airfreight would become economical only with a system designed specifically for that purpose. It is tantalizing to speculate that the paper contained an early version of a commercial aviation venture utilizing the hub-and-spokes concept, similar to the service operated for a short time by the Indian Post Office in the late 1940s. This pioneering system, according to R. E. G. Davies in his book *Airlines of Asia since 1920,* connected Bombay, Calcutta, Delhi, and Madras through a hub at Nagpur, providing overnight airmail service between the four major cities of India.

In the 1960s, the airlines were trying to figure out how to profit from the unused cargo compartments, but none of their schemes succeeded. Perhaps Fred envisioned some new approach to the future role for airfreight, but since his paper is lost to us and he has no clear recollection of the details, we can only surmise its contents. Nevertheless, this young upstart would take just over a decade to solve "the airfreight problem."

FRUSTRATING EXPERIENCES

In the fall of 1969, following his Marine Corps tour of duty in Vietnam, Fred joined his stepfather, retired air force colonel Fred Hook at Arkansas Aviation Sales, a struggling operation located at Adams Field, Little Rock's municipal airport. Arkansas Aviation provided fuel and hangar services for local and itinerant general aviation aircraft, usually small propeller-driven planes operated by independent owners.

Using funds bequeathed to him from his father's estate, Fred bought control of the business. He assembled a network of reliable suppliers, acquired a large inventory of commonly used parts, and built a reputation as a fast-response, low-cost corporate jet equipment and maintenance center.

Fred next decided to purchase corporate jets for resale. His ability to consistently provide critical parts for his corporate jet customers and his unique approach to jet aircraft brokerage transformed Arkansas Aviation Sales into a profitable entity within two years.

Behind the scenes of this smooth-running operation, however, lingered the frustrations associated with obtaining parts needed on a rush basis. The existing airfreight system was inconsistent and at times downright unreliable. It was difficult to get a clear picture of where the delays were occurring, and each entity in the supply transportation chain blamed others for slow service. A "rush" air shipment might arrive in two days or in four, or might take as long as a week—expensive and irritating delays when a corporate executive was kept waiting or had to take a commercial flight instead of traveling in his or her accustomed luxury.

Fred's experience exposed the shortcomings of the airfreight system that relied on passenger airlines and independent ground handling companies: there were too many links in the chain. In short, there was no single entity responsible for the expedited movement of goods from shipper to customer.

THE FEDERAL RESERVE

Fred was growing disenchanted with the aircraft brokerage business and the day-to-day operation of Arkansas Aviation. The business had always had a reputation for being full of unscrupulous characters who sometimes ignored ethical standards to complete a sale, and Fred was uncomfortable dealing with some of these people. It was time to seek another occupation, something more compatible with his father's challenge to him to make wise use of his inheritance.

One of Fred's early ideas was to establish a flight courier service for transporting bonds. The concept was of interest to at least one Little Rock bond house, but Fred couldn't get adequate insurance to cover the losses that might be encountered if the plane were to crash or if a pilot decided to make off with a sack of bearer bonds.

Next, Fred adapted his idea for the Federal Reserve. The process for clearing checks between banks, particularly those located in the more remote sections of the nation, was inefficient and slow, sometimes taking up to ten days, at a float estimated to be nearly $3 million a day. By examining the logistics required to move bundles of checks between the thirty-six district banks, Fred realized that the hub-and-spokes model was the only system that could accomplish the transfers within a reasonable time frame and with a manageable number of aircraft.

He conceived a plan for a business that every night would pick up checks and documents from each Federal Reserve branch bank, fly them to a central hub for processing by Federal Reserve employees, and deliver the sorted bundles to the appropriate member banks early the next morning. The Federal Reserve would benefit from the system, and he would have an interesting aviation-oriented business to manage. Because the Federal Reserve would be his only client, he proposed to call his fledgling company Federal Express.

The system would need fast, reliable aircraft to cover the distances involved in a national network; in fact, the same type of corporate jets that Arkansas Aviation was successfully brokering would be ideal candidates for the service. Fred was attracted to the French-built Dassault Falcon 20 Fan Jet. The French Air Force had used these planes during paratrooper training exercises, with the doors removed, which indicated that the design incorporated an unusually strong fuselage. Avion Marcel Dassault, the manufacturer of the Falcon had designed the aircraft as a compact, ten-passenger business jet with a range of up to 2,000 miles and a speed of up to 550 miles per hour. Pan American Airways was distributing the Falcons in the United States through their Business Jet division, and a softening market for corporate aircraft had forced Pan Am to store its twenty-five unsold planes in the Arizona desert, awaiting an upturn in the economy.

When Fred presented his idea to the Federal Reserve Board, the initial response was favorable. Confident he would have his new business and a rewarding career built around his love of flying, Fred invited his two sisters to join him in the new venture. They formed a company with a capitalization of $500,000, half from Fred personally and the rest from the Frederick Smith Enterprise Company, a $14 million trust fund set up by Fred's father in the early 1940s for Fred and his two sisters. Then Fred convinced the directors of the trust fund to guarantee a loan of $3.6 million to purchase and modify two Falcons from Pan Am. Federal Express was incorporated in Delaware on June 18, 1971.

But the positive response was not forthcoming: the independent Federal Reserve directors were unwilling to modify their schedules to accommodate the proposed service. That left the shell company with two new Falcons and a debt of $3.6 million.

THE MATURE CONCEPT

In truth, the mature plan for the Federal Express service, as with most creative ideas, did not spring forth fully conceptualized. It was in fact inspired by a series of events that over time contributed to the concept's evolution.

Fred's love of airplanes, the Yale term paper, and the frustrations associated with obtaining critical parts at Arkansas Aviation Sales all pointed to the need for a transportation system that could provide consistent, reliable, and expedited movement of critical, time-sensitive goods. Perhaps the greatest contribution to the evolution of the fully developed concept for Federal Express occurred while Fred was working out the logistics for the transportation of Federal Reserve checks and documents. By expanding upon his concept for the Federal Reserve, Fred formulated a nationwide operating system responsive to the needs of time-sensitive shippers and, as a bonus, found an intriguing way of using those beautiful corporate jets to expedite shipments.

There had been great progress in transportation since the days when the Hudson's Bay Company had promised to deliver goods to the Yukon Territory within 14 months of receipt of an order, but Smith knew the industry was ready to make a quantum leap, and he was determined to make that happen.

Although the industry seemed wary and even hostile at times, Fred would heed the advice of author, poet, and philosopher Ralph Waldo Emerson: "It is a lesson which all history teaches wise men; To put trust in ideas and not circumstances."

2

Checking with the Experts

I first met Fred Smith in December 1971. My twelve-year-long business career up to that time had been spent entirely with the consulting firm of A. T. Kearney and Company, first in Chicago and then in New York City. I worked primarily in the fields of transportation and physical distribution and, at the time, was the principal responsible for that part of the firm's practice on the East Coast.

Kearney was a very professional organization and a great place to work. Its clients included most of the major airlines, railroads, and trucking companies in America. The Kearney approach involved conducting a thorough analysis of the client's needs, development of programs specifically tailored to the client's situation, and in later years, assisting the client to implement the recommended changes. This approach demanded the maximum level of creativity from those of us working day to day, with the client's senior management. It was a challenging environment, one that guaranteed the rapid development of a consultant's management and communication skills.

One day, as I was completing a report for one of our transportation clients, our receptionist interrupted my concentration.

"Mr. Frock, there is a Mr. Fred Smith from Federal Express in Arkansas on the phone who wants to talk about a project concerned with air cargo," she said. "Can you take the call?"

"Sure," I responded, "are you certain he said 'Federal Express'? I've never heard of them. See if you can find any information about the company while I talk with him."

"OK, I'll transfer him to your line now."

This phone call was my first contact with Federal Express. Fred, after briefly introducing himself, requested a meeting for the following day to discuss a consulting assignment of some urgency relating to his plans for a new business venture.

When Fred arrived at our office, he brought with him a few of his associates, whom he neglected to introduce, and proceeded to unfold his plans. Fred had already done a great deal of homework. He appeared to understand what it would take to convert a private jet into a cargo carrier and the potential difficulties of obtaining an operating certificate needed to carry out his plans. As this erudite 27-year-old continued to describe his plan, I listened with a mix of skepticism and growing admiration. The concept, at least on the surface, was interesting.

However, Fred had no real in-depth understanding of the potential market for an overnight small-package service, the difficulty of overcoming entrenched competitors, and the genuine complexity of setting up an organization to carry out the program. In addition, there were the questions of whether funds were available to launch the enterprise and whether the venture would be profitable.

I already knew most major airlines treated cargo as an afterthought, operated as a stepchild to the more lucrative passenger side of the airline. I was certain of one thing from our past consulting work: airplanes were expensive to buy, modify, and operate. It was not clear to me at the time that an opportunity existed for a system operated with small, expensive jets to produce a profit, even though I suspected that there was a latent market need for the service. However, Fred's enthusiastic and optimistic description of the planned venture carried the day. I promised to give the matter of Kearney's involvement further consideration.

As a first step, I checked out some of his references and learned that Fred was a serious, highly respected member of the Little Rock community. His bank confirmed that, indeed, Fred possessed the financial capability to carry out his intentions, at least as far as our study was concerned. After discussing the concept with some of our senior staff members, I called a few of the more progressive transportation and distribution managers with whom we maintained an ongoing relationship. I began to get excited about Fred's concept when these independent sources related at length the frustrations they were experiencing with delayed or lost shipments.

My next job was to prepare a proposal that outlined the work to be accomplished and the approach that we would take either to aid Fred in his remarkable quest or, as I explained to my project team, to at least attempt to dissuade him from wasting his financial resources on an impossible dream. I had no inkling of what I had just agreed to do, or what a dramatic effect it would have on the rest of my life.

OUR STUDY OBJECTIVES

On December 20, 1971, I completed our proposal that outlined the approach we would take in conducting the study. We had the following initial study objectives:

1. Identify the prospective market potential by market segment

2. Identify likely users of the service by industry and geographic location

3. Identify the likely products for the service and their characteristics

4. Evaluate potential customer attitudes about the service features

The proposed venture was dauntingly complex, and our approach reflected this. Fred agreed that we should maintain close liaison with his organization throughout. If we determined the market to be viable, we would evaluate the financial potential of his concept. If the results were still positive, we would outline the service's operational requirements, relying on Fred to sketch out the air operations and related flight costs. If at any stage we became convinced that the concept was not viable, we would conclude our study and document the reasons for our decision.

3

Feeling More Comfortable

The priority airfreight market in the early 1970s was dominated by REA-Air Express (the Railway Express Agency), a company already on the decline, and Emery Airfreight, the first certified airfreight forwarder in the United States. Emery and some eight hundred other airfreight forwarders performed the ground service and consolidated shipments for transport by the certificated airlines. The airlines themselves also offered air cargo services, using for the ground portion of the movement Air Cargo, Inc., a company owned by twenty-six airlines. UPS (United Parcel Service), through its Blue Label Service, consolidated small packages for transport by the airlines, but did not provide a true priority service. The Post Office offered a "Priority" mail service that amounted to only a small fraction of the total airfreight market.

We structured our market research to include more than one hundred personal interviews backed up with a mail questionnaire to over four thousand commercial and industrial organizations selected from industries known to be users of airfreight. Data compiled by the Civil Aeronautics Board, the Air Freight Forwarders Association, the U.S. Department of Commerce, and Dun & Bradstreet were also included in the research effort.

Early in 1972 we were ready to discuss our initial findings relative to the airfreight market. Several of his associates, whom he again neglected to introduce, joined Fred at our meeting. Our major conclusions from the marketing study were as follows:

- Approximately 37,000 commercial establishments in identified target industries accounted for 86 percent of all domestic airfreight shipments.

- The growth rate for air cargo averaged over 17 percent per year for the previous six years, and the demand for expedited service still appeared to be in its infancy.

- Except for a few major city pairs, overnight delivery service was not being consistently provided, but the need appeared to be genuine.

- Airfreight shippers particularly stressed the need for complete door-to-door service, wanting to "get it out the door and forget about it."

- The total 1972 market for airfreight shipments under 50 pounds was projected to be approximately 20.4 million shipments.

- A proposed network of 111 cities would cover 95 percent of the airfreight movements in the United States.

- In view of the proposed system's uniqueness, Federal Express could expect to attract a market share of at least 11 percent, or more than two million small-package shipments annually, representing 70 percent of the total capacity of the planned fleet of operational Falcons.

Fred's concept passed the first hurdle of the study—establishing the need for the service and confirming that the market was large enough to sustain a viable business.

We were confident that after completing the national network, the superiority of the system would attract business from Air Cargo, REA, the U.S. Postal Service, UPS, Emery, and a few other large freight forwarders. Our greatest concerns related to the resources and funds needed to complete the network, and the real likelihood that the stronger established competitors would immediately copy the Federal Express system.

Other factors enhanced the outlook for the proposed service. The scheduled airlines were gradually moving away from direct point-to-point schedules toward utilizing major hubs as transfer points. This allowed for the rapid introduction of larger-capacity aircraft and provided enhanced economies for the airlines, but initially it also reduced the frequency of flights. This was problematic for the forwarders for it necessitated complex transfers, often between different airlines at the hubs.

Furthermore, recessionary pressures and the introduction of larger jet aircraft had begun a trend that eliminated over 1,500 flights per day leaving many cities with marginal or discontinued service. The increased frequency of mishandled shipments and prevalence of in-transit delays were beginning to cause a further decline in an already unreliable transportation system.

To make matters worse, several major airports began instituting curfews, restricting the time that planes could land or take off. For example, shipments from West Coast cities had to depart the originating airport before 3:00 in the afternoon in order to reach their East Coast destination prior to an 11:00 evening curfew. Transfers to other eastern cities could not be accomplished until the curfew lifted the following morning.

THE NEXT PHASE OF THE STUDY

Fred and I agreed to proceed with our study, outlining the anticipated cost and revenue structure as well as the operating capital requirements. It was obvious that changing the Falcon from a comfortable corporate jet to a rugged cargo hauler was going to require substantial time and up-front expense. Where would the funds come from? Fred—as usual, several steps ahead of us— revealed that he had been discussing with the Postal Service its need for dedicated mail routes between certain cities. He had also researched the corporate market for full-plane cargo charters.

Why not use the first modified Falcons in other revenue-producing roles until enough planes could be converted to begin the small-package operation? The idea made sense from a financial standpoint. Fred provided us with his information, and we agreed to include the possibility of utilizing the first group of modified Falcons for mail routes and charter service in our analysis.

To determine the startup capital requirements and ongoing operating expenses, we needed to look at the entire delivery network. We immersed ourselves in the system's operating procedures, including flight operations, aircraft loading and unloading, pickup and delivery functions, hub operations, communications, revenue accounting, management information systems, and staff support departments. In the process, we came to understand the advantages of flying everything to the central hub, such as the inherent simplicity of clearing all packages from each location every day, making just one sort decision for each package, and optimizing aircraft usage.

We created several pricing models to analyze the potential revenue stream, paying particular attention to the pricing structure of Emery. Emery's service was generally considered the best in the business, and we knew it would form the benchmark for Federal Express. By comparing the most realistic price models with the projected operating costs, we calculated the achievable operating income for the complete system at various levels of capacity.

The major unknowns were the time required to reach the financial break-even point and the time to reach full system capacity. These uncertainties, when coupled with the other little surprises that inevitably crop up to challenge new enterprises, would lead many potential investors to stay on the sidelines. This was not going to be an investment for the fainthearted, and was certain to separate the casual backers from the true risk-tolerant investors.

I was gradually overcoming my initial skepticism. As the study progressed, we grew to appreciate Fred's brilliance and open-mindedness. Moreover, Fred's enthusiasm was contagious. I was beginning to suspect he had the drive and leadership skills to pull this off and that his enterprise was worthy of such optimism.

4

This Dog Might Hunt!

n mid-April 1972 I arrived at the offices of Arkansas Aviation Sales to present our last progress report prior to preparing a final report. We started with a tour of the facilities and met some of the employees, most of whom were involved with sales operations and care of the corporate jets. While the offices at Arkansas Aviation were at best Spartan, the hangar area was quite a different story. Crammed into every possible parking space were beautiful, shining, expensive corporate jets of various configurations and with a variety of company logos and color schemes designed by their previous owners, which Arkansas Aviation had purchased for resale.

There was even an Aston Martin sports car parked in the corner of the hangar similar to the James Bond model. Curiosity got the better of me and I just had to ask what that beautiful car was doing parked in an airplane hangar. Fred had taken the car as a down payment in trade for one of his smaller propeller planes, as he turned his attention to the more rewarding corporate jet market. As he explained, "It takes up a lot less space than the plane."

Corporate jets were usually sold like boats, through established brokers on a consignment basis. During the recession starting in 1969, there was very little demand for used corporate jets, so the prices had fallen to historically low levels. Fred had seen that as an opportunity to purchase the aircraft for direct resale. By coupling his knowledge of corporate jets with a creative sales and marketing approach, he had managed to bring profitability back to Arkansas Aviation. It was an early indication of his ability to adapt creatively to an encountered business opportunity.

Following our tour, we settled into a makeshift conference room to present our most recent findings and to discuss the overall potential for the Federal Express concept. The process was designed primarily for the client's benefit, but also served to point out those areas that might require further clarification when we prepared our final report. We knew our report would be critical to the company's quest for prelaunch funds.

At this point, there were still many uncertainties. Our major concern was the likelihood of securing outside capital, which would drive the schedule for completing the small-package network and in turn directly influence how soon priority shippers could be convinced to use the system. Despite significant concern about the unknowns and the potential difficulties, we concluded:

- The guaranteed overnight package delivery system was operationally and financially feasible.

- With an aggressive sales force, a sound management team, and careful attention to detail, Federal Express would have relatively little difficulty reaching the break-even level of 11 percent of the selected markets.

- The initial startup operations would require additional capital investments of approximately $16 million, not including the cost of aircraft acquisition and conversion and construction of central hub facilities. (At Fred's direction, the projections assumed the aircraft would be leased in a fully modified condition, ready for all-cargo service.)

- Annual pretax earnings for the full system operation were forecast to be $7 million to $14 million within three years of instituting the complete system.

From there, we considered traditional wisdom: To begin with, a relatively low percentage of startup ventures succeed. Second, even the most promising and best-planned startups often require double the time and double the investment capital estimated during the research phases. Another challenge would be the difficulty of reaching operational sustainability—the point where the business would generate enough revenue to cover the continuing cost of expanding the service area. While the company worked to expand the service network, shippers would be asked to use Federal Express only for those packages up to 50 pounds destined for areas served by the company.

We felt it our duty to be candid about the role of the chief operating officer. In our opinion, Fred was too young to undertake that role by himself. He had no corporate administrative or operating experience. Even a cursory look at the staff of Arkansas Aviation Sales indicated that the firm lacked the management talent necessary for the job that lay ahead.

AN UNEXPECTED OFFER

Realizing that attracting experienced aviation-oriented and logistics business talent to Little Rock might be difficult, I offered the services of A. T. Kearney's executive recruiting group to assist with the task. Fred's thoughtful response: "Executive recruiters will take too much time. You've already done all of the background research, designed a basic operating plan, developed a financial forecast, and outlined the structure for the management group. Why don't you just come here and make it work?"

It was an entirely unexpected offer, and one I should have found easy to refuse. I was happily employed by a highly successful and well-respected organization, in a responsible supervisory position with at least a reasonable shot at becoming a managing partner within a few years. I had a steady income from work I enjoyed, a comfortable office in Midtown Manhattan, a fine home in Westport, Connecticut, and a growing family. Fred was proposing that I trade all that for an uncertain future with an organization in Little Rock that existed primarily in the creative mind of a young entrepreneur.

Yet common courtesy and good business judgment required that I not react too critically to Fred's offer. After a short hesitation, my response was, "I appreciate the offer. I will think about it and let you know my decision." It was the only time in our nearly five-month relationship that I had not been entirely candid with Fred.

On my flight back to New York, I mulled over Fred's offer. The potential for an exciting business experience was certainly there, and on a few previous consulting assignments, I had actually functioned in the capacity of a chief operating officer until the client could locate a replacement. The experiences had been a refreshing departure from the standard consulting assignments, but I couldn't help thinking that filling that role on a temporary basis for an established organization was vastly different from pulling a rabbit out of the hat every day for a startup like Federal Express.

Furthermore, certain characteristics of Fred's personality were troublesome. I intuitively felt that while he possessed great leadership potential, he apparently had little regard for the people around him. I reasoned that if he had considered his associates important, he would have at least introduced them at our meetings—a small thing, but to me an important omission. I wondered how he might treat his staff.

No, the situation just did not feel right. On returning to the office, I began drafting the final report, planning to end my contact with Fred on a high note. Fred could distribute the document to the financial community and use it as a blueprint for his future operations. It would then be up to him to sweat through the problems and get his operations off the ground.

5

An Irrational Decision

The following week Fred was in New York and had some people he wanted me to meet after work. Later that day at a Midtown Manhattan hotel, I was introduced to Art Bass and Vince Fagan. Fred then proceeded to explain that Art and Vince were consultants from the Aerospace Advanced Planning Group. *They had just completed a study to evaluate the potential market for the proposed Federal Express service!*

I had no clue that another team had been working on a study, duplicating at least a part of the research we had been doing. Trying to conceal my astonishment, I calmly probed to find out more. Fred had first become acquainted with AAPG when Art was making a sales presentation to Little Rock Airmotive, the neighboring airplane modification center on Adams Field. The month before Fred first contacted Kearney, he authorized AAPG to determine the size and nature of the market for priority small packages and to recommend the most effective way to structure a marketing program for the service.

Art and Vince were confident in their assessment of the market but practical in their appraisal of the proposed venture. It seemed odd to me to have two independent groups developing information on the size and nature of the market; however, as I was later to learn repeatedly, Fred was anything but a conventional businessman.

Vince, a former marine with the build of a soccer player, was a marketing expert with a hard-nosed approach to promoting products and services. Art, also a former marine, was tall, handsome, unassuming, and immediately likable. He appeared more of a generalist, convincing in his overview so long as you did not push for too many details. Prior to forming AAPG with Vince, Art had been the chief pilot for New York Airways, a helicopter operator shuttling passengers between mid-Manhattan and the New York area airports. I later learned that he was the first person to land a helicopter atop the Pan Am building, inaugurating commercial service from that location. That probably accounted for at least some of his easygoing personality. As Art himself explained, after the experience of that first approach and touchdown, other situations just did not seem quite as critical. The two made an interesting team.

While the Kearney study focused on the operational and financial segments of Fred's venture, the AAPG study concentrated on developing the most effective way to structure a marketing program. Simply stated, Kearney outlined the means to service the market; AAPG focused on the way to market the service. Fred had just provided the first demonstration of his unique ability to move quickly and unconventionally through the basic planning elements and to compress the time needed to get his operation off the ground.

Art and Vince underscored their findings that 80 percent of the small priority shipments originated in or were destined for cities outside the country's twenty-five largest markets, while airlines were decreasing service to the smaller passenger markets. They also concluded that 90 percent of the nation's airliners were out of operation between 10:00 at night and 8:00 in the morning. Even more astonishing, AAPG had determined that at least one hundred large to medium cities were not receiving any overnight service. This represented an enormous opportunity for Federal Express. The challenge would be to have the adequate financial backing to implement such an extensive national network.

The conversation then turned to the future and the interesting, if daunting, task of making the proposed venture a reality. Fred, as usual, was passionate about his idea, ready to take on the world.

"What about funding?" we asked.

"No problem," he responded. "I already had a preliminary meeting with a well-known investment banker here in New York who will raise the funds we need." Then, unable to resist ribbing Art and Vince, Fred continued, "In fact, they were the ones that suggested having the research done by a respected firm like Kearney instead of you flying saucer guys."

Unruffled, Art queried Fred on his approach to overcoming the Civil Aeronautics Board restrictions that limited the routes commercial airlines flew and the rates they charged. Fred was reluctant to discuss the details of his plan but assured us that he was confident of overcoming those restrictions.

CONFRONTING MY DOUBTS

Leaving the hotel, Fred confirmed that he was indeed ready to begin assembling the staff to move ahead with the next phase of his proposed venture. He confided that Art had already agreed to join the venture, and pressed me for a decision on his previous offer. Realizing that he was now serious, I promised to give him an answer after the upcoming weekend.

All the normal fears went racing through my mind: How could I even consider joining Fred and his crazy scheme? I had a mortgage and a commitment to my family. I did not even know anything about housing or living in Arkansas. What about the schools? We had three children who needed a good education. Did they even have good schools in Little Rock? If I were to accept the job, perhaps I could commute to Federal Express and come home on the weekends. That was what consultants did anyway.

I was short on actual operating experience, but I was, as our professors declared, a qualified master of business administration; I could do the job. I had already turned down two promising offers to run established companies. Was I too comfortable to take a risk on a new venture? If I did not make this leap, would I regret it for the rest of my life? With all of my doubts, there was something really compelling about the situation. The thought was seductive. It was insane!

I rationalized that providing operational assistance to Federal Express would not be significantly different from consulting for the company. Then I thought about Art. In our brief meeting, I could sense the warmth and compassion he would bring to the management group. He would provide a wonderful balance to Fred's more rigid temperament. I also knew that Art's broad vision and mellow personality would be tremendous assets for Federal Express. I found that encouraging.

Before the end of the following week, I made my decision to join the great adventure, but did so more from intuition than from logic. The decision was also made without serious consideration of my family, something I would later regret.

To make matters even more bizarre, I was going to accomplish this great feat with a considerable cut in pay. When my friends asked why, I really could not think of any logical reason. There are times when we just are motivated to do things for reasons that we don't clearly understand; perhaps for the thrill and risk of the unknown, or to rekindle the spirit, or because it is time for a change, or because some unrecognized mysterious power is providing direction to our lives.

At this point, I could not help but marvel at the twists and turns that ultimately affect our lives; the events and people that shape us in ways that we seldom appreciate and never clearly understand. The persuasive Mr. Smith had introduced me to another fork in the road, and this time I would follow Yogi Berra's unforgettable advice, "When you come to a fork in the road . . . take it." I would select an uncharted path toward an unknown destination. The experience would change me in ways that I could not have imagined. I decided to put all doubts out of my mind, to ignore all of the logical reasons for continuing my comfortable career with Kearney (figuring that I could always get a real job in a year or two if Federal Express did not succeed), and to become a part of Fred's fanatical vision.

On May 12, 1972, I officially joined a very select group of Federal Express employees, with my three-year employment agreement to serve as general manager and chief operating officer of a company with little, if any, real concept of the difficulties that lay just over the horizon.

6

Kick the Tires,
Light the Fires

Fred was never one to wait around for things to happen. Near the end of the consulting study, Fred began searching for an agency to develop a professional corporate image and logo. At his request, I made several calls to New York firms, but the best price I could get was over $100,000, and that was just too expensive. The company was still months away from startup, and Fred decided to defer development of the corporate image while he attended to other more pressing matters.

Then fate stepped in. Rick Runyon, a young designer from Los Angeles, flew his own airplane, a Cessna 310 to Little Rock on a mission to convince Fred that he was the one to create our corporate image. Rick had his own West Coast graphics company and was responsible for the branding for Getty Oil. He now wanted to do the same for a new airline in need of a dramatic, eye-catching image. Fred was somewhat skeptical, but Rick offered to do the whole thing at his own risk and charge a fee of $25,000 only if Federal Express used his design. It was a generous offer, and one that Fred was pleased to accept.

Rick returned several weeks later with sketches of the Falcon painted in different color combinations. The sketches, hung on the wall of Fred's office, became objects of discussion. Each new visitor was asked to pick his or her favorite. The overwhelming favorite was the purple, orange, and white combination. When Fred asked about a logo, Rick replied, "With your budget, you should not be trying to get people to understand a complex logo.

Just use the name of the company and the new lettering I've created emphasizing speed and motion." Rick got his money eventually, and the purple, orange, and white paint scheme became emblazoned on every plane and vehicle.

CHALLENGING AVIATION REGULATIONS

Fred continued to push ahead with the preparatory activity that would lead to the inauguration of the small-package service. Near the end of December 1971, shortly after our first meeting in New York, Fred had executed an option to purchase twenty-three additional Falcons from Pan Am. Then, early in 1972, backed by loans from local banks, Fred purchased eight used Falcons, reasoning that he could always sell the planes for a profit through Arkansas Aviation Sales if the existing regulations stymied his plans for the small-package service.

Fred had good reason to be concerned about regulations. The airline industry of the early 1970s closely resembled a public utility, with government agencies overseeing the routes airlines could fly and the rates that could be charged for passengers and cargo. These regulations and restrictions, which applied not only to passenger airlines but also to any commercial aviation enterprise, would have a significant effect on our new company. Federal Express in turn was to play a noteworthy role in reexamining the premise of this prototypical New Deal regulatory structure.

The 1926 Air Commerce Act was the cornerstone of the federal government's regulation of civil aviation. The government considered airline service essential to commerce and regarded regulation as necessary to protect the public interest. Based on the record of the Post Office airmail routes from 1917 to 1926, which produced "200 crashes, 43 deaths and 37 serious injuries," the act also reflected the need to protect the lives of participants.

Beginning in 1938, all air carriers needed a "certificate of public convenience and necessity" in order to operate. The airlines operating at the time—American, Delta, United, TWA, Eastern, and eighteen other carriers—were automatically issued certificates. The Civil Aeronautics Board (CAB) was then established in

1940 and empowered to approve and disapprove fares, control mergers and acquisitions, determine the routes on which certificated carriers could operate, and specify the types of cargo a plane could carry. Transfers or abandonment of route certificates could occur only with CAB approval. An airline could not go into or out of business, or do anything in between, without permission from the CAB.

The Federal Aviation Act of 1958 created an independent Federal Aviation Agency, which later became the Federal Aviation Administration (FAA), with broad authority to combat aviation hazards. To transport passengers or property by aircraft as a common carrier for compensation, it was necessary to obtain two separate authorizations: *safety* authority in the form of an Air Carrier Certificate from the FAA and *economic* authority from the CAB.

REGULATIONS GOVERNING AIR TAXI OPERATIONS

There was an exception, however, that governed air taxi operators (small airlines operated for compensation and hire with aircraft having fewer than twelve passenger seats and a maximum takeoff weight between 12,000 and 27,000 pounds). Air taxis were exempt from CAB regulations. Federal Express needed to become an air taxi before it could operate planeload charters free of CAB oversight.

The FAA's influence was total, affecting every facet of an airline's operations. Air taxi operators were required to conform to all safety and operating regulations mandated for certificated carriers, with the exception of the need for a cockpit voice recorder, a flight recorder, and other minor operating considerations. Other companies had already certified the Dassault Falcon 20 for use in charter operations. For the FAA to award us an air taxi certificate, we had to show how the business was going to operate; the FAA would then determine whether our plans were proper and safe.

Federal Express's chief pilot, George Eremea, and the head of maintenance, Dick Yarmowich, prepared the initial flight and operating manuals that described our operation, and filed the application. The FAA ultimately approved it and issued Operating Certificate No. SW-LIT-140T to Federal Express on March 7, 1972.

There was one slight problem: engineering modifications on the first two Federal Express cargo Falcons increased the maximum gross takeoff weight to 28,660 pounds, 1,660 pounds over the limit allowed in the CAB regulations for air taxis. Three days after receiving the FAA operating certificate, Federal Express applied to the CAB for an exemption to the existing weight regulations, pleading that the company would otherwise be prohibited from using the modified Falcons. Federal Express argued that it was now an approved air taxi operator, that it intended to commence planeload charter operations using the modified Falcon, and that no increase in carrying capacity resulted from the engineering modifications. On April 3 the Civil Aeronautics Board granted the exemption, but this was just our first glimpse of the often harrowing nature of the bureaucratic process.

Now it was time to cast aside all doubts, charge ahead, and get on with the program—borrowing from one of Fred's favorite phrases of jet jockey jargon, it was time to "Kick the tires, light the fires; hi, ho paint, let's get where we ain't."

PART II

Naïve Optimism
May 1972 to March 1973

7

A Climate of Chaos

In my 12 years at A. T. Kearney, I had adjusted to the realization that corporations rarely conducted their operations in the crisp, professional manner we had presumed in the business school classroom, but even the more disappointing consulting experiences had not prepared me for the chaos I encountered at the Arkansas Aviation Sales facility.

Irby Tedder, a retired air force colonel, was the executive vice president, controller, and "mother hen" of the group. He was well qualified for his role at Arkansas Aviation. Irby had served as inspector general of the Continental Air Command and as commander of two large air bases. The "Colonel," as he was frequently addressed, had amassed over 8,000 hours of command pilot experience and served as deputy wing commander in the Strategic Air Command, which operated B-47 jet aircraft.

Irby was a calming and mature influence on the group, but in some respects, the staff was almost unmanageable. He described Fred as "a nitpicker who had his hand in everything. He worried about seemingly insignificant problems that other people could easily have handled." However, after my first few days of "managing by walking around" and just observing the confusion, I concluded that Fred had a right to be concerned about the trivial problems. People were doing a lot of talking but had no idea of the enormous tasks required in the next 10 months to launch our small-package service.

Irby knew the shortcomings as well as the capabilities of the Arkansas Aviation staff and felt that with proper direction, they could be motivated to get the job done. Irby frequently had to act as a buffer in my dealings with the employees. He helped me understand the limitations of the people placed in roles entirely foreign to them. I was expecting this tiny, naïve staff to perform functions they were not equipped to handle.

Fred was great at explaining his vision and defining the direction for the company. However, there was no coordinated management effort to ensure either was followed. Irby confided to me his opinion that the people around Fred did not know how to manage anything. They needed better direction and a more structured environment. They needed to become an informed, organized operating group.

Irby was right. There were plenty of ideas about how to prepare for the future; the problem was that each person had his own idea of how to put Federal Express together. In those days I was continually reminded of Peter Drucker's sage advice: "The executive's job is to get the right things done; management's job is to get things done right." It was going to be a monumental task.

FIRING UP THE FAA

Several of the Arkansas Aviation employees transferred to the Federal Express payroll. Fred had selected George Eremea as director of flight operations, based on outstanding experience, including his record as a test pilot and former aviation manager for Arkansas governor Winthrop Rockefeller. A graduate of the Air Force Test Pilot School, George had flown the F-80 in 1949 and progressed to the F-104 fighter jet. He had over 3,000 hours as pilot-in-command for Falcon aircraft.

George had been modifying the flight operating manuals for several weeks prior to my arrival, while Dick Yarmowich rewrote the maintenance manuals. These manuals were the final prerequisite needed to begin planeload charter operations for the postal service and other commercial customers. Fred suggested that I attend the coordination meeting between the FAA representatives and our staff to see what I could do to speed up the process. The manuals were nearing completion, but at every meeting, the FAA required additional changes before granting its final approval.

Having had no chance to review the manuals, I had no idea what information they contained, much less the nuances of the FAA's requirements. I felt that George, Dick, and the FAA could figure out the correct material and wording to satisfy the regulations. There was no need for me to get involved in that detail; I just wanted to get the task completed.

I reminded everyone that we had a business to run, and asked the FAA inspectors to give us a list of the corrections needed to obtain their final blessing. The FAA representatives seemed somewhat perplexed, but agreed. Our small staff worked diligently to make the appropriate modifications, and two weeks later, we met again.

The FAA approved our modifications at this point, but its request for yet more changes came as an unwelcome surprise. Somewhat irritably, I reminded the representatives of the urgency of this work, concluding, "This is a matter of trust. We trust you to respect your commitments just as we must honor our promises. We are willing to make one final attempt at satisfying your requirements, but deferral beyond that point is totally unacceptable." At the next meeting, with final approval of our manuals, we had FAA authorization to proceed with the charter operations.

I did not realize until years later how brash and downright risky my actions had been. One evening while walking through our maintenance hangar, one of the FAA inspectors stopped me to comment on the growth and progress at Federal Express. We had a pleasant conversation about current operations and the company's rosy future. The talk eventually gravitated to a discussion about Federal's early struggles, especially in the regulatory arena.

This inspector had been part of the team present at my first coordination meetings. "You know, no one had ever talked to the FAA in that manner, and we just did not know what to think," he said. "We were doing our best to speed the approval, and as it turned out, you received your final authority in less than half the normal time." I suddenly was thankful for small miracles and the higher power that protects the uninitiated.

PROFITING FROM A ROBBERY

I spent much of the late spring of 1972 designing the management structure and determining the key players needed to carry out our operating plan. We prepared so-called best- and worst-case operating forecasts for the financial community. We considered the operating and reporting requirements needed to run the business and began preparing for the July startup of the charter flights and mail contracts.

Little Rock Airmotive (LRA) was doing the prototype modifications based on Dassault's design specifications. Meanwhile, George was testing the operating characteristics of the cargo Falcon, using sections of railroad track to simulate the weight of differing package loads. On one occasion, it seemed to me that he had an unusually large amount of track for the test flight, so I questioned the weight of the rails. He smiled and said, "We are testing to the maximum cargo capacity of 6,500 pounds." Then he reminded me of the adage "There are old pilots and there are bold pilots. There are no old, bold pilots." "I am testing to the outer limits," he said, "but I do expect to live to a ripe old age."

As I walked away, I had a nagging suspicion that George was about to conduct an unauthorized test to make certain the plane could operate safely even if it somehow became slightly overloaded.

The A. T. Kearney study broadly described the early operational structure and the steps needed to launch small-package operations. As a means of tackling these tasks, and to inject some discipline into the atmosphere, I assembled the staff and assigned each member a list of projects. I scheduled regular staff meetings to redefine the scope of the work and to coordinate the ongoing activities. Then, using a rudimentary form of management by objective, I required follow-up reports.

My actions were not always popular, and a few of the workers clearly resented my structured approach. Several complained to Fred that the staff meetings were spent determining the status of assigned projects, questioning schedules, uncovering reasons for delays, and discussing alternative approaches to meeting our objectives. Excellent! The staff at least was getting a good grasp of exactly what we needed to accomplish in a short time. Fred supported the changes.

I was now commuting between Little Rock and Westport, going home each weekend in a rhythm that was entirely familiar from my consulting days at Kearney. One Monday morning, I learned of some unusual excitement the previous Saturday. While the staff was busy working, a masked gunman entered the facility, ordered everybody into one office, and demanded all their money. Fred, never one to carry cash, had only a dime in his pocket. He turned this over to the nervous robber while trying to calm him, concerned that his revolver might accidentally discharge. Everyone else emptied their pockets, but the gunman, apparently unaccustomed to his weekend career, was shaking so badly that he dropped some change on the floor. A quarter rolled toward Fred as the robber fled the scene.

Fred calmed the others and promised to reimburse their lost funds. Then he picked up and pocketed the quarter, thereby making a profit of fifteen cents. I felt if he could make a profit from a robbery, we somehow were destined to make the company a success.

Fred, Irby, and I continued preparing highly detailed financial projections for our own in-house use. Together, we expanded on the material in the A. T. Kearney report, assembling forecasts of the venture's imaginary workforce and operating needs on a month-by-month basis for the remainder of 1972 and all of 1973. This startup business plan would lead to the beginning of small-package operations in the spring of 1973 and the projected expansion of the service to a nationwide system by the end of that year.

It was an optimistic forecast, but it appeared feasible. Certainly there were some risks, but we thought they were manageable. We saw a clean slate and imagined the ideal world. We would find a way to lease more Falcons; we would get the remaining restrictive regulations modified; we would assemble the necessary talent; we would have no difficulty getting financing. We would provide the fastest and most reliable service in the business. Customers would jump at the chance to ship with us!

As we sat back to admire our work, Fred said, "This looks promising, but if things don't go according to plan, we can always arm the ten Falcons and take over a small island somewhere in the world." But we really didn't want to think about that alternative. We were convinced the small-package concept was magic. We were all terribly optimistic. We were all appallingly naïve.

8

Looking for a
Few Good People

The development support staff needed to be experienced, creative, flexible, and capable of moving quickly in order to have the system ready in less than 12 months. Most of all, the staff would have to be compatible and work in harmony. This was to be no place for egos to disrupt the flow of accomplishment. Only a group of dedicated individuals could pull off this Herculean task. It was going to take a significantly larger and more sophisticated staff than the one we had at Little Rock in the spring of 1972.

Irby continued to be a valuable source of information, providing knowledgeable insights into the personalities and capabilities of the small staff from Arkansas Aviation Sales while serving as a stable bridge between the corporate jet activities and the hectic pace of the Federal Express startup. It sometimes seemed as if everything needed for the small-package operation required a unique approach; we were not merely reinventing the wheel, but creating an entirely new type of service that had no direct precedent.

Ted Weise was about to join the new staff. Born in 1944 and raised in central Ohio, Ted studied electrical engineering at the Missouri School of Mines and Metallurgy. "I learned to fly in college and almost flunked out because I enjoyed it so much," Ted admits. The first company he worked for went bankrupt, and he was laid off from his second job. While looking for new employment, he contacted the regional head of the FAA in Memphis, who told him, "Boy, do I have something for you. You need to call this kid over in Little Rock. His name is Fred Smith."

"I finally arranged a meeting with Fred," Ted recalled, "and started in with all this stuff about loving airplanes and wanting to be involved in aviation. Fred cut to the chase in an instant. He said, 'Damn it, I want somebody who wants to make some money.'"

Fred arranged a visit at Little Rock Airmotive. "In the hangar were two unpainted and a few used Falcons in corporate configuration," Ted explained. "People were tearing them apart, ripping the leather seats out of one and cutting a big hole in the side of another one. My jaw just dropped to the floor. I figured Federal might become another big aviation bust or an incredibly worthwhile adventure, but either way, I wanted to be a part of it."

Near the end of April, Irby called Ted at home with an offer, stressing that a slot had just opened. Ted hesitated and said, "Well, I won't be able to make it for at least another week and a half." After a short pause, Irby said that was acceptable.

Ted remembers that he then suddenly got a sick feeling. He had asked for the week and a half only because it was turkey season and his father-in-law was teaching him to hunt wild turkey. Irby was willing to wait, though, so Ted finished turkey season, went to Little Rock, and started working in the flight-following department.

Ted and his colleagues set up the system to monitor the progress of our planes. They had the flight crews phone in as they prepared to depart from each airport. A large display board in the front of the operations room showed the progress of each plane compared to the scheduled flight plan. It also provided management with information on the status of our air operations and our developing network.

CHARTER AND MAIL RUNS

At the beginning of July, Fred and I traveled to Baltimore, where he convinced Commercial Credit Equipment Company (CCEC) to provide Federal a 10-year loan to replace the short-term local bank loans hastily arranged for the first group of Falcons. The loan was backed by a mortgage on the planes, a pledge of $2 million collateral from the Enterprise Company, and Fred's personal guarantee.

Earlier, Fred had sent an Arkansas Aviation Sales employee to research the postal service's need for supplemental service. He discovered that cutbacks by the regional airlines were causing serious delays, and that the postal service was planning to solicit bids from air taxi operators for scheduled nightly full-plane charters. Fred decided to bid on the routes. The airmail contracts required service only on weeknights, so the aircraft would be available for commercial planeload charters during the day and on weekends.

We were awarded several round-trip routes, returning to the point of origin each night: Indianapolis-Cincinnati–New York; Chicago-Buffalo-Pittsburgh; Dayton-Columbus–New York; Cleveland-Buffalo-Pittsburgh-Atlanta; St. Louis–Cincinnati-Baltimore; and Columbus-Baltimore. The two new Falcons and the eight used planes covered by the CCEC loan were ready for service on the mail and charter runs or were nearing the end of the extensive modification program across Adams Field at LRA. Mail routes began in July and required an on-time completion of 96 percent. With all six routes in operation, the mail runs generated revenues of just under $300,000 per month.

The new, hydraulically operated cargo door simplified the loading and unloading operations. The modified avionics package provided all-weather reliability and allowed the flight crews to operate in a scheduled airline environment. The mail runs were proving our ability to provide a dependable service.

Commercial charter operations served another purpose during this heady time. We recruited corporate jet salespeople from Arkansas Aviation Sales to call on major companies in need of small-plane charter service. These contacts introduced us to Ford, General Motors, IBM, Hughes Tool Company, Avon Products, Polaroid, Union Carbide, Western Electric, Abbott Labs, RCA, and others in the Fortune 500. The charter service started out well enough, steadily growing from 14 flights in July to 141 charters in December. However, we were beginning to get a dose of reality. We were attaining only 45 percent of our expected charter revenue, and the situation deteriorated further in the following year.

We were able to respond quickly to emergency requests for transportation, but it was not a particularly good bargain for our customers. The Falcons were new, sleek, and fast, but older turbo-prop planes were a much better value for the higher-volume shippers like the automotive companies. Except for charters under 6,000 pounds, the Falcon was just not competitive.

BUILDING THE MANAGEMENT TEAM

My first move to assemble a new management group was to contact an old friend and former A. T. Kearney associate, Michael Basch, a business administration graduate of Clarkson College of Technology who had spent eight years at United Parcel Service, working in virtually every functional group, including sales, customer service, operations, buildings and facilities, and industrial engineering. He had also worked with several project teams opening new territories for UPS.

Mike left Kearny because he couldn't bear the two-hour bus commute from New Jersey to Manhattan. He went to Grand Rapids, Michigan, to work for Rapistan Technics, a company-owned consulting group specializing in material handling and distribution. I contacted Rapistan to help design the handling system for our Memphis hub. Mike knew most of the details about every project that Rapistan was doing, except the Federal Express project, which his boss was treating like a top secret.

Coincidentally, following a visit to Rapistan, Mike was booked on the same originating flight. This was his opportunity to find out something about the Federal Express project. In response to his questions, I described the things we were working on, adding that I was looking for someone to head sales and customer service. Mike said, "How about me?" I thought a moment and invited him to visit Little Rock.

The following week, Mike got to see some of the hectic activity in the hangar area in Little Rock. Over dinner, I gave Mike copies of the consulting studies and promised to meet the next morning to discuss the material. Later that evening, Fred called to notify me that we were going to Dallas the next morning, so I invited Mike to come along.

"Our conversation on the way down was very casual and low-key," Mike recalled; "then I saw Fred's presentation. He was more than impressive; he was captivating. I found myself hoping that somehow they would give me the opportunity to be a part of the adventure."

Starting the third week of September, Mike Basch, then just three weeks shy of 34, joined our group of crazies. The pay was not much, but he became senior vice president of customer sales and service. That would at least look good on his next résumé if things did not work out. It was fascinating to see how excited people could get about the company. A passion seemed to permeate everything and everyone.

Fred and Irby also continued recruiting other new additions to the working group. By the end of September, the Federal Express roster listed forty-two employees. Included on the list was John Tucker Morse, our in-house counsel, and Norm Timper, head of flight operations.

"Tuck" Morse grew up in Little Rock and received his law degree from Hastings College of the Law at the University of California. When he returned to Little Rock, Tuck took a job clerking for a federal district judge. "Fred came in to testify as an expert witness," Tuck recalled. "My clerkship was up in three or four months, and Fred offered to pay me what I was making with the federal government." Tuck joined the company in August 1972.

Norm Timper helped Federal Express set up flight operations. He had retired from United Airlines after 34 years, and his long experience in flight operations helped us to develop professional standards for the flight group. At the end of September, the flight and maintenance group included twenty-three people, more than half of the company's employees.

Our next challenge was to set up a computer-based data processing system. We would need a sophisticated system. I toyed with the idea of hiring an outside firm to handle that part of the operations. Then I remembered Leon Tyree, the systems and programming manager for Jones Trucking Company in Spring City, Pennsylvania.

I had worked with Leon on a consulting job to design and produce an innovative management information system at a time when many other computer departments were limiting their output to accounting and financial data. We were going to need additional information to help us track the Federal operating systems.

Leon arrived in Little Rock near the end of the summer and immediately started putting together a plan for our data processing operation. "My first priority was to figure out how to keep up with the maintenance statistics on the Falcons," Leon said. "The next challenge was to get a billing program running in less than seven months, before the start of small-package operations. I quickly hired Wes Terry, and we selected the Burroughs 2700 computer because it was excellent at running Cobol programs, it was cheap, and it was available right away."

THE VA FLIGHT SCHOOL

Meanwhile, the company had to focus on its primary goals. Federal would need many more qualified pilots as the small-package service rolled out. Numerous pilots were returning from military service in Vietnam, but Federal Express flight crews needed to be experienced in commercial operations and also to be type-rated in the Falcon aircraft—more specifically in the Federal Express cargo version of the Falcon. So we decided to open our own training facility.

Our Veterans Administration–accredited flight school opened in Little Rock during September 1972. The school was always booked with a waiting list of candidates numbering in the hundreds. The school was a win-win situation for everyone: Returning veterans used the GI Bill to become type-rated in the Falcon, the program provided badly needed operating funds for the company, and Federal Express ultimately hired most of the pilots trained at the facility.

I loved to watch the landings and learned how to identify the pilot's former experience. The ex–air force pilots, accustomed to long runways, made very smooth touchdowns well past the beginning of the runway. The former navy and marine pilots, accustomed to landing on carrier decks, seemed about to crash at the very beginning of the runway. The challenge was to break old habits and create a standard of performance somewhere between the two extremes.

I had almost forgotten Fred's assurance after the New York meeting that Art Bass was joining Federal, but Art finally arrived in October. I was elated that this genuinely likable aviation specialist really was joining Federal. After his Marine Corps tour, Art had established AAPG with Vince. Art, then 40, was giving up his consulting practice and plush Sutton Street apartment on Manhattan's East Side to help bring Fred's vision to reality. It was a good omen . . . we couldn't all be nuts! We were going to succeed.

Our new management team now had to focus on the March 1973 startup. This was a once-in-a-lifetime opportunity to revolutionize the transportation business. We were on the threshold of a new era—preparing to play a unique role in the birth of the information age. We were inspired, but we still had much work to do on other critical matters.

9

Mr. Smith Goes
to Washington

Our air taxi exemption for planeload charters did not license us to operate the small-package service. Regulations then required any airline operating aircraft with a maximum takeoff weight in excess of 12,500 pounds to obtain a certificate of public convenience and necessity (CPCN) from the CAB—our Falcons had a maximum takeoff weight of 28,660 pounds.

Application for a CPCN typically required three or four years during which the applicant had to state exactly what it was going to do. Existing certificated airlines could, and regularly did, oppose the introduction of any new service simply by maintaining it was not needed. Furthermore, the CAB had *never* granted any airline the broad authority we were seeking. The certification route was not a viable alternative.

Our only option was to seek a change in the regulations. Fortunately, there had been some promising activity in that direction. In January 1972 the CAB had proposed a new exemption for air taxi operators based on the number of passenger seats and cargo payload capacity. Several aircraft manufacturers, about a dozen air taxi passenger carriers, Federal Express, and a number of small communities filed comments in support of the proposed change, and as expected, several larger airlines and the Airline Pilots Association (ALPA) filed comments in opposition.

We argued that the 12,500-pound weight limit had been formulated in the DC-3 era and did not take int account advances in small-aircraft speed, range, and capacity. Our opponents alleged that the CAB lacked the statutory power to expand the venue of the air taxi operators.

The entire future of Federal Express depended on the outcome of these hearings. So how to remove this impenetrable roadblock? Fred called me into his office and announced, "I have decided to go to Washington to gather support for our position. You remain here and keep things moving."

Fred joined the group lobbying for new regulations, providing supporting testimony, and suggesting an increase in the weight limit for the cargo portion of the exemption. The CAB ultimately decided to adopt the proposed changes; by September 1972, authorized air taxi airlines operating aircraft with less that thirty passengers or with a maximum payload under 7,500 pounds were exempt from economic regulation. Maximum payload for our Falcons was 6,500 pounds. Now we could operate when and where we decided, exempt from CAB regulation of our rates and routes.

This was an enormously important decision for Federal Express. *Without this change in regulations, we'd never have gotten our first package off the ground.*

ANOTHER ROADBLOCK

We thought our regulatory problems were over. Then, ALPA and the airlines petitioned the U.S. Court of Appeals to reverse the CAB's decision. Time became our enemy once again—the Court of Appeals would take at least a year to reach a decision. If we began operations before the final decision and the court reversed the CAB decision, would we then be fined and forced to cease operations? We needed an informed opinion on the possible outcome of the case. Robert Murphy, a member of the CAB and its former vice chairman, recommended we talk with Nat Breed.

Nat had begun his law career as an attorney with the CAB, and ʾr the direction of its members, had written the board's deci-
ʾhe new exemption case. In the latter part of 1972, Nat left
ʾ join a small law firm. "When I was first contacted by
ʾs," Nat recalls, "Airlift, Flying Tigers, and Seaboard
ʾl-cargo carriers, and they had just taken a bath.

Then along comes Federal Express, which is not only going to go into the air cargo business but is going to limit itself to small packages, and it is going to fly very expensive twin-engine corporate jets. It sounded like a crazy idea!"

Nat, putting aside his personal feelings about the wisdom of the venture, agreed to a luncheon meeting with Fred and Frank Watson, one of Federal Express's attorneys. Frank, a cross-examiner by nature, honed in on the one issue that was uppermost in our minds—what was the likely outcome of the attack on the amendment. Specifically, Frank wanted to know Nat's thoughts on how the court was going to respond to the appeal, especially since the CAB had recently been reversed on an exemption case and rebuked by the Court of Appeals for failing to pay attention to the boundaries of its authority.

Nat felt that the CAB was acting within its authority when it granted the air cargo exemptions. If the Court of Appeals did reverse the CAB, he said, they would do so with instructions for the board to grant specific relief to any organization that changed its position or invested money in reliance on the ruling's validity. In other words, Federal could continue to operate as if the decision were upheld. When Frank heard that, he breathed a sigh of relief.

Fred was now confident that we could push ahead. We immediately began working with the FAA to modify the operating manuals to include small-package operations. Nat was correct in his assessment, and the Court of Appeals later upheld the CAB's decision. Providential timing and good fortune had coalesced to remove another roadblock.

Next, we needed to acquire the remaining Falcons from Pan Am. However, we could not find a leasing company willing to undertake the risk of the venture. The funds to purchase the remaining Pan Am planes would therefore have to come from the private placement—another troubling dose of reality.

By mid-September, Pan Am was pressuring us to take the remaining Falcons. The airline had held the planes off the market for nine months and wanted its money. However, we hadn't found our backers yet, and Pan Am finally relented, granting us a delay until the first week of November in exchange for an increase in the purchase price.

A month later, Federal Express still didn't have the money. We negotiated a second delay, agreeing to take the remaining Falcons by January 31, 1973, naturally at a further price increase.

A NEW LOCATION FOR THE CENTRAL HUB

A lot of thought had gone into the central hub concept and the advantages of sorting all packages at one central location. Originating cities would simply load all packages on the single plane destined for the central hub. Our intensive training and checking programs would virtually eliminate sort errors. At the hub, we could also match package volumes to plane capacity and reroute flights as needed while still maintaining schedule integrity. The central hub was simply the most economical way to operate the system and the best way to achieve consistent reliability. The question then became, Where should it be located?

Initial studies favored a city at the center of gravity of the small-package market. The hub also needed to be far enough south to escape heavy winter storms and far enough north to be away from the most severe summer weather, especially tornados and hurricanes. Fred and I visited all of the locations that matched our basic criteria, looking at commercial airports and active or abandoned military bases. Eventually we narrowed the candidates to Little Rock; Smyrna, near Nashville; and Memphis.

Little Rock had several drawbacks. Adams Field had only one runway equipped for instrument landings and had no available space for our sort hub. Fred appealed to the Little Rock airport authorities to help correct some of the deficiencies, but got nowhere. Smyrna, an abandoned air force field, was better suited to our flight requirements, but lacked facilities and a community infrastructure—that is a strong local labor pool and adequate housing for our employees.

Memphis was ideal. The airport had parallel instrument runways north and south as well as east and west. Ned Cook, chairman of the Memphis airport board, offered us three hangars across the field from the passenger terminal and acres of ramp space, and even proposed to finance a new sort facility and administration building with a 20-year general revenue bond. The surrounding area could provide labor for the hub, and the town was an attractive and mature community, perfect for our central headquarters. It was good-bye, Little Rock—hello, Memphis.

Fred was concerned about Arkansas congressman Wilbur Mills's reaction to the decision. Mills, head of the powerful House Ways and Means Committee, had provided assistance through his contacts in both the regulatory and financial communities. Fred made a personal call to Mills and told him of the decision. The congressman was initially surprised and perhaps a little annoyed, but as Fred pointed out the benefits of Memphis, Mills understood that the move was just a business decision driven by financial and operational considerations. He continued to support the company.

Ted Weise had worked for a while in Memphis, so Fred assigned him to work out the details of the transfer to the new city. Ted was thrilled with the assignment because "Fred trusted me. There was nobody looking over my shoulder or telling me how to do the job."

The management group and almost everyone else shared Ted's feelings. Fred was very good at setting goals, identifying the things that needed to be done, and having absolute faith that his people would complete their tasks. He wanted progress updates, but he never questioned whether you were going to get the job done. He just expected it.

The Humble House Gang

As we started to look at the enormous task of establishing the ground pickup and delivery operations, Fred began thinking about ways to shortcut the process. One alternative was to form a joint venture with United Parcel Service. Basch contacted UPS and set up an appointment with Jim McLaughlin, the chief executive officer.

"What are you guys doing here?" McLaughlin asked.

Basch responded, "We have an appointment."

McLaughlin said he didn't have the meeting on his calendar, but graciously invited our delegation to the conference room. Fred described what he had in mind and the role he would like UPS to play. McLaughlin abruptly said, "No, we're not interested in doing that."

McLaughlin's indifference turned out to be a "save" for us. If UPS had agreed to become the ground distribution arm of Federal Express, it would have controlled the customer base and, most likely, the priority package business. Federal Express, if it survived at all, would probably have become just the air portion of UPS.

MORE STAFF SUPPORT

Meanwhile Mike managed to attract several more former United Parcel employees. The UPS imports shared two apartments at the same complex in Little Rock, which we labeled Humble House. Mike, Art, and I shared a third unit.

Mike, in need of additional help to train and motivate the ragged sales group, turned to Ted Sartoian, a former colleague who had boosted sales for UPS. Ted had recently left the company to open a restaurant in Fort Lauderdale. Mike explained his situation and asked, "Who do we sell to, how do we sell to them, how do we find their hot buttons?"

"I'll help you with that," Ted responded, "if you hold all your meetings down here."

Our sales, customer service, and key field operating personnel headed for Florida the second week in January.

We had just 100 days to get everything in place for the inauguration of the small-package service. "At the Florida meeting, we got everyone to understand what had to be accomplished, how we would set up service to our first cities, and what we would have to do to have to reach our target customers," Mike explained. However, we were soon to learn that the Federal Express prospects had different expectations from the typical United Parcel customer.

Meanwhile we had other problems. Several of our sales people, formerly from the corporate jet world, were accustomed to dealing with an entirely different type of client and they had difficulty relating to the UPS methods for selling the small-package service.

Dennis Sweeney was so intrigued by Mike's description of "the United Parcel Service of the air" that he joined the Humble House team in January 1973. Dennis, 31, had worked for Mike at UPS in Philadelphia. Taking the least expensive flight we could find for him, he left New Hampshire at 8:00 in the morning; was routed from Manchester to Keene, New Hampshire, and then through Cleveland, Detroit, Chicago, and Memphis; and arrived in Little Rock close to midnight during one of the worst ice storms of the century.

We'd chosen the Memphis airport for its exceptional reliability. We touted it to our investors. For all but 15 minutes in the ten years prior to 1973, Memphis would have been safe to land with the avionics we had installed in the Falcons. However, the same freak ice storm that greeted Dennis crushed our invincibility argument. The storm coated the entire area from Memphis to Little Rock with up to three inches of ice. Dennis called his wife the following day. "These people are out of their minds," he told her. "We're iced in and I've done nothing but sit here and read manuals. I'm thinking of packing up and coming home."

However, Dennis stayed on and modified some old UPS procedures, features of service, and rate charts to make them look like Federal Express material. He became a jack-of-all-trades, working anywhere needed, and in the often haphazard, helter-skelter bustle to launch the small-package service, he was key. "If this is an indication of how organized you are," he said, "I think we're in deep trouble."

Next, Dennis worked on the field operations, defining the responsibilities of city locations, which we called stations. He prepared manuals describing the processes for handling outbound packages and sorting the inbound packages. He also developed a protocol for loading packages on the delivery vans and making customer deliveries.

Federal Express hired *courier-salesmen* (they were not just truck drivers) and required them to maintain a neat appearance, be courteous, and use the customer's front entrance whenever practical (the rear loading dock was for truckers—UPS, Emery, and REA Express). We expected our couriers to be part of the sales force, comfortable communicating with secretaries, receptionists, and mailroom clerks in addition to the shipping managers. Dennis's work formed the foundation of a basic training program for the new station personnel we were about to hire.

Dennis visited Adams Field, met Fred, and got to see one of the Falcons. That plane, the first to complete the modification cycle, had been painted with the tail number N8FE. The number 8 was significant: With airbrush techniques the 8 was changed to a 3, 6, 9, and 5 for duplicating on our promotional materials, showing our "extensive fleet."

Dennis was then assigned to the presales task force formed to identify the target cities for the March runs. After his first meeting, he recovered from his initial impressions and shared in the excitement as Art, Mike, and others from the Humble House group began outlining their plans for the start of the small-package network.

The target cities for the March startup fell into two groups. There were five originating cities—Atlanta, Kansas City, St. Louis,

Nashville, and Memphis—picked primarily because of their close proximity to the central hub (we did not need planes for the latter two cities). Customers in these five cities could ship packages to each of the other four originating cities plus five destination-only cities: Dallas, Greensboro, Jacksonville, Cincinnati, and Little Rock. The sales force concentrated on identifying and meeting with prospective shippers in the five originating cities.

It was a very limited system. We could dedicate only two Falcons to the service. Six of the planes were committed to the mail routes, at least one was required for scheduled maintenance, and as a conservative measure, we reserved one as a backup. We figured that if the beginning package volume exceeded the capacity of the two planes, we could activate the spare.

It was critical at the outset that we establish a high level of reliability. Each plane could carry 450 to 500 packages, and we just could not afford to leave any behind. By selecting originating cities near the Memphis hub, we could run the inbound route twice if demand exceeded our capacity. As an added precaution, we scheduled the hub sorting time for three hours.

We ignored the fact that Federal Express was an unknown entity and that the onus would be on our customers to isolate packages weighing less than 50 pounds and those headed to recipients within 25 miles of our ten destinations. Instead, we focused all our hopes on providing a truly superior service. We were cautiously optimistic.

11

Good-bye, Little Rock—
Hello, Memphis

While Mike was conducting the Florida meeting, he and Ted Sartoian talked about the heady days of expanding UPS's service areas and the sales blitz teams that had been so successful. Mike decided to duplicate that approach for opening the new cities at Federal Express. Ted suggested hiring an experienced high-level manager to take responsibility for the field operation. He recommended Mike Fitzgerald, then vice president of operations for the D. H. Overmeyer Company in New York, the largest public warehousing and warehouse leasing company in the nation. Ted knew Fitz very well and said, "This is the guy you need to get on board."

Mike contacted me several times," Fitz recalls, "but frankly, after UPS I had enough of small packages to last me the rest of my life. The business was horrible around Christmas and other holidays. I told Mike there was no way I was going to move to Little Rock. My wife, Joan, and I were living with our two children in a beautiful home in Ridgefield, Connecticut, on an idyllic two-acre setting with a stream, wonderful neighbors, and excellent schools. I was content with my job at Overmeyer and I wasn't going to leave all of that."

Somehow, Mike managed to lure Fitz to our Little Rock offices for a tour. "When I walked into that office space that looked like an old garage, I was tempted to turn around and beat a hasty retreat back to New York. It was really scary," Fitz recalls. "There were three or four tiny offices and everybody was sitting on top of each other."

Mike knew that this former UPS manager would fill a critical vacancy in his organization, so he made certain that Fitz received the royal treatment; everyone worked hard to convince him of the rosy outlook for the company and the major role he could play in its success. Fitz, especially after seeing our facilities, remained reluctant to consider leaving his secure job in the Big Apple.

"Fred turned on the charm in a way that few others can match," recalls Fitz. "He started talking rapid fire about the industry, explaining things very eloquently and believably. However, some of the things he said struck me as being extraordinarily naïve. I was not sure he understood all the practical matters, but I could sense he was determined to find people that might make up the shortfall."

Then, Mike contacted me to arrange an interview. Fitz was an attractive and immediately likeable individual with an Irish sense of humor and picturesque speech. I was interested in his qualifications and the contributions he could make, immediately and longer term.

I learned that he had also been in the marines. We were getting enough marines to form our own platoon. Fitz had joined UPS in 1957 as a driver in Watertown, Massachusetts, and within a year became the area manager for Connecticut, Massachusetts, and Rhode Island. Later, he became an instructor at UPS's basic training school for supervisors and rose to manager level there. He also served as operations manager for the company's northern Illinois district, supervising more than 1,000 drivers and hub employees. That was pretty impressive.

After our interview, Mike took Fitz to the hangar across the street to see a newly painted Falcon. The hook was set. Fitz caught the bug that had bitten the rest of us. That evening, he called his wife and said, "I think that this might be a good opportunity." Joan replied, "Look, don't kid me; you have already accepted this job in your mind."

Ted Sartoian was correct. Fitz was precisely the person we needed to assume responsibility for our fledgling field operations. In February he moved into the already crowded apartments at Humble House and became our vice president of package operations. Like almost everyone else at the officer level, he accepted a pay cut with promises that things would get better in the future.

As the time approached for the Memphis launch, Art and I turned our Humble House apartment over to Mike and his expanding group and moved to an even humbler location in Memphis. One evening a friend of Art's was passing through town after attending a New York City going-away party for a local character named "Hot Suit" Harry, who had just been convicted of robbery and sentenced to 10 years in the state penitentiary. Art's friend considered our shaky enterprise, looked around our modest dwelling, and pronounced, "You know, Hot Suit really has it better than you guys—at least he knows when he's getting out."

The flight operations and maintenance groups moved to Memphis early in January. We now had acres of ramp space and three underutilized pre–World War II hangars. The ground level of Hangar 7, the center building of the three, would serve as the interim hub for a few weeks while the new hub sorting facility and administration offices were under construction. Except for the VA training program and Little Rock Airmotive, which were to remain in Arkansas, we completed most of the moves well before the planned startup.

The senior management group operated from the upper floor of Hangar 7, which offered a welcome respite from the crowded conditions of Adams Field. Fred's office, located above the temporary sort area, featured a badly worn floor in front of his desk with a hole large enough to observe the activity below. We covered the hole with a rug when we were expecting visitors.

12

The Company Lodestar

Federal Express has always valued its people; it is the proper and equitable thing to do, and from a business perspective, good employees, vendors, and customers are valuable assets, not easily replaced. Debra Howse is typical of the high caliber of the people who contributed to the company's success. The story of how she came to be a part of this exciting venture is a tale of compassion and caring, excitement and anticipation, and another of the amazing "coincidences" that seemed to surround the building of the core group at Federal Express.

Shortly after Debra settled into her new job at the Adams Field ticket counter, a new customer handed her his air travel card. It read "Fred Smith, Federal Express." Debra reasoned that with a common name like Smith, he was just a regular employee with an ordinary job. She had seen the colorful planes during lunch. Thinking she might buy some stock, she asked Mr. Smith if he knew anybody at Federal Express to help her.

"Mr. Smith seemed puzzled at first," Debra remembers, "but he was polite and then with a smile replied, 'Well, I know a few people. Here's my card. Call me when I get back from New York, and I will introduce you to some people who can help you, but the first people to have stock in Federal Express will be the employees.' I took the card, shoved it in the pocket of my uniform, and never looked at it because I was writing his ticket—I knew his name."

"About two weeks later," Debra continued, "Fred called and asked me to come in to see him. We must have spent two hours together. He was impressed with my personality and said that if Federal Express were to succeed, it would require positive people. He recognized something in me that I didn't see in myself and offered me a job, saying someone would call me."

Fred later had second thoughts about hiring Debra. During the interview, he learned that she was a widow with two young children who was struggling to make it on her own. Fred realized that it might be unfair to take her away from the security and stability of American Airlines.

"In fact, Fred told Mike Basch not to hire me," Debra said, "because he didn't want me stuck in Little Rock trying to support my kids if Federal Express didn't succeed. No one at American ever cared about my situation. I was just overwhelmed by Fred's compassion and by the atmosphere of the company. From then on, if you cut me, I'd bleed purple—the color of Federal Express." Debra, an African American, notes, "Federal had gender and racial equality and opportunity long before they became buzzwords. Fred was from the South, and he could easily have taken a different route when it came to hiring. But that's not who he was."

PEOPLE, SERVICE, PROFIT

After the move to Memphis, Fred brought our tiny staff together to thank everyone for their dedication to his dream. It was a heady, exciting time for everyone present. In his inimitable way, Fred seemed to address each attendee individually, making a personal commitment to each person in the group. His speech went something like this:

> This will be a fresh, fast-paced company that cares about its people, where teamwork is the norm and everyone pitches in to contribute to its success. You will be treated with respect, honored for your dedication, and acknowledged for your special contributions. Each one of you is a vital member of the team with an important job to do, a job just as critical to the success of the company as every other job.

You will be recognized as the expert on the job you are doing and will be free to use your creative talents to improve that activity. We will provide training for your benefit, promote from within, and commit to a no-layoff policy so long as the company survival is not at stake. You will receive a fair wage for your work; you will have a protective benefit package including medical, dental, sick leave, and disability coverage, as well as a retirement plan, all of which will expand as Federal Express matures. Each of you will share in the profits of the company, and at some future point you will have an opportunity to own stock in the company.

Thus was born the FedEx policy to honor and reward its impassioned employees, the *people* factor. Fred continued to the next part of his speech, explaining the *profit* factor:

Each of you, doing your job to the best of your ability, will produce a strong company with a surplus to reinvest in our future. The surplus will fund wage increases, provide for a profit sharing program, and ultimately provide your retirement benefits. Profits will also provide a fair return on invested capital for our shareholders. This dedicated core group is going to make Federal Express a model for other companies to emulate.

Mike then spoke about the *service* factor. The company was dedicated to providing the highest level of reliable service humanly possible, irrespective of the difficulty of maintaining that service. This was our typical way of moving forward—Fred pointing the way (leadership), executives supporting and expanding on the vision (management), and motivated associates eagerly carrying out the plan (implementation).

Thus was born the company mantra, the lodestar, the guiding ideal, and the primary foundation of the corporate culture at Federal Express—motivated *people* working together to produce exceptional *service* for customers who would provide revenues to produce *profits*. The genesis of the cultural vision was beautiful in its simplicity, it was motivational, and it was accurate—*People-Service-Profit*, the trinity of cyclical action.

In *Customer Culture: How FedEx and Other Great Companies Put the Customer First Every Day*, Mike Basch writes, "Culture drives performance in an organization. Put an average human being in an above average culture and the person will change behaviors to adapt to the new culture. Build a culture where the behaviors you desire are clear and recognized and people will gradually build habits around those behaviors. Then the organization will habitually serve its customers with ever increasing value."

Mike then uses my favorite concept of the CEO. He explains, "Vision is the compass of the enterprise . . . it is the experience the organization is attempting to create for its *Customers, Employees, and Owners*." Mike's CEO is an amalgamation of those relying on the organization, the embodiment of the organization and all those who rely on it. This understanding of our constituency was critical at Federal Express. We measured corporate excellence by how well we satisfied the often conflicting expectations of these divergent groups.

CUSTOMER SERVICE EXCELLENCE

Guaranteed on-time service and complete customer satisfaction have always been the unconditional goal at Federal. The commitment to superior service was perhaps best expressed this way: *Never promise more than you are able to give; always give more than you have promised.* This declaration was another of the company's underlying principles, a cultural value understood by every Federal Express employee.

Peter Schutz, whose advocacy of ethics in management has earned him worldwide acclaim, was a frequent visitor to our executive offices. This former chief executive officer of Porsche, in his book *The Driving Force: Extraordinary Results with Ordinary People,* concludes, "A business culture built on excellence will most frequently outperform a culture in which success is the singular objective. Managers striving for excellence and quality tend to be patient because their focus is on the longer term."

At Federal Express, the focus was not on short-term material accomplishments or quick success regardless of the long-term consequences. Instead, the cultural goal of the company was to reach a level of excellence that produced positive results for the future.

For Fred, excellence meant continually looking ahead and acting to help Federal Express meet its service commitments.

Remembering his first Thanksgiving in Memphis, Dennis recalls, "Before dinner, we went to the hub, where we found Willard Baldwin, the Memphis station manager unloading an airplane by himself. The plane, loaded with Polaroid cameras destined for Timex in Little Rock, developed a mechanical problem, so it did not fly until Thursday morning. My kids, my wife, and I started helping to unload, when Fred appeared. He was in his office working and saw us, so he came down to the ramp. Together we finished unloading the plane while Willard got a rental truck to haul the cameras to their final destination."

"After we finished," Dennis recalls, "Fred gave us a free tour of his new office. The walls were covered with drawings showing Federal Express taking over that entire side of the airfield." Fred was already thinking of the future with an expanded network and a larger fleet of planes—the drawings had DC-9s and every other large airplane imaginable.

13

More Obstacles

The commitment to take the remaining Falcons from Pan Am was just two weeks away, but Federal Express was running out of funds and facing a financial crisis. We had fallen behind on the payments to Little Rock Airmotive for the earlier conversions, and the modification center was holding back on the parts stored for the conversion of the remaining planes. Two important suppliers were threatening to close the door on the company, and numerous others were sending menacing messages about past-due bills.

We'd underestimated the capital required for the launch, thanks to the following surprises:

- Our initial plan assumed we would lease planes fully modified. We instead had to purchase the Falcons and fund the modifications ourselves.

- The delay in securing outside funding forced us to take loans at onerous interest rates.

- The funding delay also caused financial problems at Little Rock Airmotive.

Fred had come up with the initial startup funds. He had done a remarkable job in Washington, convincing the regulators to modify the outdated air taxi restrictions. His charisma and enthusiasm had inspired nearly a hundred associates to pursue his dream. The company would be ready to begin small-package operations in just a few weeks. This was not the time to fold the cards and leave the table. This was the time to ignore the problems and charge ahead!

The fastest and most direct way to solve the Airmotive problem? Just buy the company. The owners of Airmotive had two choices: They could either accept a generous cash offer or keep the Falcon parts and materials and declare bankruptcy. Fred convinced the banks to finance the purchase, and the owners were delighted to receive substantially more than the appraised value of Little Rock Airmotive.

Solving the Pan Am problem was a larger and more painful challenge. Pan Am was angry and unyielding, threatening to exercise its right to sell the remaining Falcons in the open market. Our final agreement at the end of January committed Federal to take all of the remaining Falcons by mid-May 1973 and awarded Pan Am warrants for the purchase of Federal Express stock. It was just another of the numerous obstacles along the road to success.

OUR INVESTMENT BANKERS

In February 1973 Fred, now facing the very real possibility of a failed startup, executed a best-efforts agreement with the investment banking firm of White, Weld & Company to raise $20 million, which the firm optimistically expected to accomplish within 60 days. Fred had first been introduced to Buck Remmell, White, Weld's vice president, in the fall of 1971. Buck reviewed the consulting reports, monitored the company's progress in the regulatory field, and by the latter half of 1972, sent Homer Rees to Memphis to assemble company information for a private-placement offering.

White, Weld's vice chairman and resident Chicago partner, Henry W. "Brick" Meers, undertook the challenge to raise additional investment capital for the company. During March, Brick Meers and Fred traveled all over the country in an effort to interest venture capital groups in the project. They met with little success.

On a few occasions, I accompanied Fred on his visits to potential investors. Fred would make almost the entire presentation, referring to me only to assure his audience that he indeed was assembling a management staff to execute the plan. I was on static display for the benefit of the money folks. On one occasion, the venture group brought in a young analyst who eagerly pointed out that the assumptions contained in the financial projections failed to consider the state and local fuel taxes. Fred, finally reaching the boiling point in his frustrating quest for funds, said, "Anyone who is not smart enough to figure out that airlines do not pay state and local taxes on the jet fuel they consume does not deserve to be an investor in Federal Express." With that, he gathered up his papers and said to me, "Let's get out of here; we have better things to do."

We would begin without a strong promotional program and without the necessary long-term funds, but by now, Fred was absolutely convinced that investors needed to see the small-package service in operation before they would provide the necessary capital.

REFINING OUR SALES PITCH

While Fred and Brick conducted their frustrating search for private investment funds, Mike sent his "Sales Blitz Teams" out to begin the sales effort in originating cities. Each team had a leader supported by a group of four to six sales representatives. Armed with credit cards, city maps, industrial directories, and lead-prospect cards, each salesperson canvassed an assigned territory and made sales calls each day. Evenings were devoted to evaluating prospective customers' reactions and discussing ways to improve sales effectiveness. In addition to acquainting shippers with the new service, we were seeking feedback from prospects so that the system would reflect and meet the expectations of the priority small-package shippers.

We changed the characteristics of the service offering almost every week after receiving the feedback from the salespeople. Each week Mike would review what the sales force learned and make adjustments to reflect what the customers were saying they needed. We were promoting *Priority One,* our overnight air service with a promise of next-day delivery before noon. We were discussing *Standard Air* service, a lower-priced offering with second-day delivery. We were touting our unique *Courier-Pak* service, which for an all-inclusive prepaid fee of $5 provided the shipper with a legal-sized envelope for door-to-door next-day delivery of documents.

Our sales force was made up of former UPS employees and former corporate jet salespeople. The UPS mentality was very conservative—watch every penny. At the other end of the scale, the corporate jet group was accustomed to riding around in limos and selling prestigious multimillion-dollar luxury vehicles. There was a serious cultural clash between the two groups. We needed an entirely new sales approach, one that lay somewhere between the extravagance of the limo riders and the parsimony of the brown company. As we progressed, we changed a few of the prevailing attitudes and developed a standardized sales approach specifically for the priority small-package shipper.

QUESTIONING THE SALES REPORTS

Every night, sales leaders from each of the originating cities phoned in an account of the day's activity. We recorded the anticipated packages reported by the sales teams, discussed the problems, provided more sales leads, and continued moving forward. The count of anticipated packages eventually rose to 3,000—much more than we anticipated!

If we had 3,000 packages, we had to cancel mail contracts. Even by flying a double turn to each originating city, we did not have enough capacity to handle that many packages. We just had to be certain that we were getting good information. That is where Mike really learned the difference between the reported success and reality.

Mike began checking out some of the more optimistic sales reports. In one case, there was a forecast for twenty packages a day from a company that made bricks. Mike naturally assumed that they were samples going to architects, but the sales representative confidently explained that the bricks were going to construction sites! That was all Mike needed to hear. After questioning all the sales leaders, he concluded we were getting what the sales group thought the management group wanted to hear.

Fitz was also feeling concerned about the package projections. Working closely with Dennis to develop the requirements for the upcoming test, he relied on the daily sales reports to extrapolate the demand for handling systems, vehicles, facilities, and staffing requirements. He recalls, "About the third sales forecast session I attended, the hair on my neck went up. There was something not right about it. It was as if this thing was just too easy."

The sales group defended its projections, saying, "This is a different business. We have our own planes and that is a powerful attraction for the urgent shipper." Fitz was getting even more antsy when he talked to people outside the company. They could not see the need for the new service, did not believe that our service could really be faster and more reliable, or did not want to trust their critical packages to a new carrier. When Fitz explained to one prospect that we could move a package from Boston to California overnight, the executive responded, "That's great, but why would you want to do that?"

In response to queries from Fred and me, Fitz responded that he could not in all conscience lease vehicles and hire people at the field locations based on the numbers the salespeople reported. He did not believe the reports and couldn't get any confirmation of their numbers. Fred finally said, "Well, Fitz, you seem to know what you are doing; go with your best judgment."

Mike and Fitz scaled back the projections by 90 percent—from 3,000 down to 300 packages. Fitz correspondingly reduced the plan for vehicles, staff, and other variable elements, but retained a backup plan just in case the volume exceeded the new forecast. We could handle the reduced package projections with no problem, and by the time the volume did grow into the thousands, we would be ready.

Meanwhile, the prospective customers were continually giving us valuable new information. We were learning more and more about the priority small-package shipper and becoming convinced that these packages were indeed special. As we continued receiving input from prospective shippers, we modified our service offerings and the ancillary parts of the service. In *The Driving Force*, Schutz accurately describes what we were experiencing: "If you listen closely enough, your customers will explain your business to you."

We began moving away from the UPS approach toward tailoring our service to the unique needs of the priority small-package shipper. Prospects were generally welcoming, even though they were apprehensive about this new kid on the block and reluctant to believe our promise of consistent, reliable overnight service. Emery, Airborne, REA Express, and every other company in the air express business was making the same commitment, and no one was able to provide the promised service consistently. Shippers that truly needed fast, reliable service were generally frustrated and often desperate—the good news for us was they were willing to try Federal Express.

PART III

Within an Inch of Failure

March 1973 to May 1974

14

Let's Call it a System Test!

Our major concern on launch day—March 12, 1973 —was the limited capacity of our small fleet. The discounted reports from the sales staff still indicated that we could expect between 300 and 450 packages. Fred was especially worried that we wouldn't have enough capacity to handle all the packages and that we would disappoint the customers. In addition, the White, Weld and Company principals were coming to Memphis to observe the first night's operations. The private placement offering was taking much longer than expected, and any hint of service failures would be disastrous.

At least we had a contingency plan: If we had a higher volume than expected, we could do a double run to our originating cities. The mail planes, after completing their runs, could be ferried to Memphis to carry additional packages to destination cities. We were not going to leave a single package behind; in fact, we were ready to give more than we promised. Our team would deliver every single package before noon the next day.

Ever more conscious of our precarious financial situation, the constant search for investor funds simply had to take precedence over the thrill of watching the long-awaited launch. So the day we inaugurated service, Fred, Mike, and I left for New York City, convinced we would have an impressive story for the potential investors we were meeting early the next morning.

As we arrived in Manhattan, Fred suggested, "Mike, while we get our bags and arrange transportation to the hotel, why don't you call and see what the volume looks like."

Basch found a pay phone and came back with the news, "It looks like it's going to be a little light."

"What do you mean a little light?" Fred questioned.

"Well, we don't have all of the reports in yet," Mike responded, "but we definitely don't need to be concerned about exceeding the fleet capacity."

"Call them back," ordered Fred. "Tell them I want the actual figures as soon as they are available, and tell them we'll call back when we get to the hotel."

On the cab ride to the hotel, we discussed the meaning of the light-volume reports. We rationalized that Federal Express, after all, was a new and unknown entity to the shippers. Perhaps we expected too much for the first day. Conceivably, the shippers did not yet fully comprehend our unique system. Had our sales force properly explained the differences between our self-contained network and the competition, which relied on multiple outside entities?

We were each beginning to feel a little less assured, less confident. Was it possible that our expectations were still too high? It was understandable that shippers would have to try our service before they made a complete switch. Surely, we would have at least two hundred packages. That would be acceptable for the first day's operation—not great but we could live with it!

The unbelievably disappointing news came with the next phone call. Our first day of operations did not produce two hundred packages, not even one hundred packages. The actual number was . . . six packages!

"Are you sure that you understood correctly?" Fred demanded.

"Yes, I double-checked; the number is six," responded Mike. Now here was another dose of reality, a really serious dose!

We just looked at each other, too numb to speak, then retired to our rooms. The three of us spent a sleepless night wondering what we were going to do next. Having heard these results, we immediately began referring to the March startup as the "system test." We did not mention our first run at the investor meeting.

This abortive start nearly shattered our feelings of invincibility. It was painful even to think about that night. It was like a bad dream, only it was not a dream. All that work, that careful planning had produced just *six packages*! Were we all idiots?

It was a hard lesson for all of us. We had ignored one of the fundamental rules of good management by not contacting some of the potential customers to check out the validity of the reports. Yes, we had reduced the sales estimates by 90 percent but then had fallen into the trap of expecting 10 percent of an unrealistic number.

I thought we had failed Fred, but it would take more than a disappointing system test to derail Federal Express. True, the test was frustrating to all of us, but it forced everyone to face reality. From this point on, we would follow the advice of Winston Churchill: "If you're going through hell, keep going."

General George S. Patton had equally good advice for our situation: "Victory and defeat are rarely absolutes, and there is a whole spectrum of degree between these two extremes." Failure is part of business; it will happen. "The time to intervene is not when things are going well," Patton maintained, "but when they are in trouble. It takes courage and character to engage a faltering project."

Fred was about to demonstrate his courage and character.

The Marine Corps
Boot Camp Mode

The "system test" network generated so few packages that we decided to cancel the flight schedule and place the packages on commercial airlines. We did not fly planes in the package system again until the next startup. It was a matter of reducing our operating expenses and conserving our dwindling supply of funds.

The daily volume from the five original cities averaged only about ten to twelve packages. Later we developed sophisticated analytical tools and ran the program to understand more about the test network. We discovered that the expected volume between all ten original cities was only forty packages per day for the penetration level we anticipated. The analysis also showed that each new city added to the network raised the volume levels geometrically. We were facing the classic chicken-and-egg dilemma: Federal Express needed an expanded network to reach higher volume levels, and an infusion of funds to expand the system to a level of sustainability.

THE PRESTARTUP ORGANIZATIONAL STRUCTURE

In March, Charles Brandon joined us as our vice president of operations research. With his wrinkled corduroy jacket, worn blue jeans, and long rumpled hair, Charles was our technical wizard, the stereotypical absent-minded professor. Our management structure was constantly in flux throughout the early years; flexibility and fluidity were its main characteristics. There was no hierarchy, just a partnership of equals.

We continually added to the management staff, often without a clear understanding of where the new hires would fit within our loosely structured organization, and generally at a salary well below their expectations. Fortunately, the group worked so well together that a rigid structure was unnecessary and titles were virtually meaningless. Our new additions were attracted by a love of aviation or the excitement of a new venture and were hooked by the enthusiastic entrepreneurial spirit.

In lieu of large salaries, most new hires received big titles: vice president, director, or manager. This left us with no choice except to designate the upper echelon as senior vice presidents. In the spring of 1973, we formed our first formal organization and distributed organizational charts, just like a real company. Until that time, everyone more or less had understood the organizational relationships, but now we were adding remote locations and were about to reshape the company.

It is probably worthwhile here to recap our organizational structure as we were setting out to reinvent the company. We preferred a broad, flat structure that positioned senior executives within easy reach of the front-line employees. Fred of course was president, with me, the general manager, reporting directly to him. The group senior vice presidents reporting directly to me included Mike, Sales and Customer Service; Norm, Flight Operations; and Art, Planning. Irby, who headed Administration and Finance, reported directly to Fred. Under the senior executives were group vice presidents and managers.

The truth was that the senior executives all worked for Fred, but we were free to make our own decisions on how to execute the overall plans. During his frequent absences to meet with potential investors or testify on regulatory matters, we kept things moving forward. With the exception of our weekly executive staff meetings, where we coordinated our activities, he did not spend time looking over our shoulders. Fred was much more interested in what needed to be done next. He was always looking far ahead of the things the management group was struggling with day-to-day. We accused Fred of operating on a different clock than the rest of us: He frequently proposed new approaches or refinements beyond our existing technical capabilities, but his instincts were usually right.

FIVE WEEKS TO RESTRUCTURE OUR NETWORK

After the March system test, Fred switched into Marine Corps boot camp mode. He assembled the entire management staff, and after expressing his displeasure in his finest drill instructor manner, calmly explained that we were now going to reinvent Federal Express. "We are going to do it right this time," Fred explained; "failure is not an option." This was leadership in action. We would be ready for the formal inauguration of service to an expanded number of cities on April 17, in just a little over four weeks.

Since Art assumed responsibility for selecting cities for the expanded network, he immediately contacted his former partners at Aerospace Advanced Planning Group in New York, Tucker Taylor and Vince Fagan, to provide manufacturing and airline data. Charles, Dennis, and others ironed out the details for the expanded service. Fred and I held the review sessions.

Charles explained the process this way: "We had a limited number of aircraft, a limited number of hours in the day, and limited capacity. We had to figure out how to optimize our assets. That is a classic operations research problem. We picked cities with real potential that would give us the best financial return. We did that first research problem using my HP 35 calculator for the complex math. Tucker brought a copy of the CAB emplanement statistics to complement our copy of the AOPA [Aircraft Owners and Pilots Association] airport guide and the OAG [Official Airline Guide] flight guide, so we knew where the certificated airlines operated evening and nighttime departures."

To find the best candidates for our service, the task force searched within the Standard Industrial Classification (SIC) codes for industries producing small, time-critical items with substantial intrinsic or financial value. Our prime candidates were the replacement parts for the equipment installed in factories, offices, and medical facilities, 90 percent of which were developed after the Second World War. Next, the group examined employment statistics for the candidate industries within each standard metropolitan statistical area (SMSA). That helped us to identify cities with the largest potential need for our service.

Next, the task force looked at each city's airline service level and assigned a ranking based on the number and frequency of destinations receiving direct service. Using all of the information at hand, Charles designed a model that no one would ever think of doing by hand today. However, at that stage in our development, we did not even have access to a computer for the analysis. We found out that places like Rochester, New York, had tremendous demand but very poor service; that was the kind of city we wanted to add. We continued to use refined versions of this process, dubbed BPI (Buying Power Index), to select new cities for our network during most of the early expansion years.

For the April service network, the task force selected twenty-five cities within a reasonable distance of Memphis. The new network included the ten original cities plus Chicago, Cleveland, Columbus, Dayton, Detroit, Indianapolis, New Orleans, Miami, Milwaukee, Moline, Newark, Oklahoma City, Philadelphia, Pittsburgh, and Rochester. The senior management staff quickly reviewed the recommendations and focused all resources on preparing for the formal commencement of service on April 17.

Each department prepared its own plan to support the expanded network. Norm's group prepared flight schedules, maintenance plans, and new bid lines for the pilots. Mike directed the sales effort for the new cities. Irby managed the administrative, legal, and financial support for the expansion. Fitz and Dennis led the push to acquire facilities, courier vans, supplies, and station personnel in the various cities. Some of the facilities were not ideal, not places where customers would be invited to visit. A few sites were not even on airport property, but we got permits to drive on the airport ramps at those locations.

Our flight crews already had something of a uniform, familiar to most of them—heavy-duty leather flight jackets. This time, we wanted everyone in direct contact with customers to be wearing a uniform, but there was no time to settle on a design and get the uniforms produced in the correct sizes and distributed to the outlying cities. Our solution for the station personnel, salespeople, and customer service agents was less elegant but more practical given our circumstances: a white shirt, brown slacks, tie with purple and orange stripes, and tan corduroy blazer, all of which were readily available from our convenient supplier, the local Sears store.

Federal began running quarter-page display ads in the sports section of the expansion cities' local newspapers to solicit telephone responses from prospects. Ads also ran in trade magazines read by shipping and distribution managers. Direct mail to 15,000 company presidents, vice presidents, and purchasing managers in the service areas supported the ads. Our Customer Information Center contacted all respondents and forwarded leads to the field sales representatives. Our official startup of the small-package service was going to be dramatic. We would convince the venture capital groups to invest in our organization.

We were certain that expanding the network was going to give us a much better shot at success. We had enthusiastic, dedicated people who worked incredibly long hours. There were no "special people" in the organization, because everyone was special. It is hard to explain what it was really like to anyone who did not experience those times and events.

"Fred, back in those days, was bigger than life," remembers Dennis. "I don't think too many people have pulled off anything more impressive. There was nobody like him. He had that knack of inspiring people to do things that they might not really feel comfortable doing." The dedicated people of Federal Express responded to his call, and in just over 30 days, they totally repositioned the company.

An Inauspicious Beginning

We needed to show our potential customers that we were very different from any other shipping service. We tried to keep things simple by providing representatives with a sales talker, a Dick and Jane story: These are our planes, these are our trucks, this is our system, here is our sorting facility. Our system was so simple, so unique, and so new that it required explaining. Our sales group put up posters of the Federal Express planes in each prospect's shipping area as a reminder of our closed-loop system, but that still wasn't enough.

In the early days, people had a difficult time understanding the concept of shipping through the hub. Diane, one of our customer service agents doing telemarketing at the time, was explaining to a prospect that our central sorting hub was the reason we were so reliable.

The prospect said, "You mean that if I ship a package from Milwaukee to Chicago, it has to go through Memphis?"

Diane responded, "Look, sir, if you don't tell your customer, we won't. It just will be there by noon tomorrow. Will that work?"

The prospect was quiet for a moment, apparently thinking over the merits of Diane's suggestion before answering, "OK, I'll ship!"

At this point, everyone was making sales calls. I phoned a Detroit-area distribution manager I knew from the days at Kearney when we cochaired a session at an annual meeting of the National Council of Physical Distribution Management. I explained our system and convinced him to try our service. A few days later, he called to say he had shipped packages to ten different locations and was pleased that we delivered all the packages before noon. He was excited by the service, explaining, "I shipped to addresses where we were having problems, and that is the best service I have ever had to those locations. Count on me to use your company for all of our urgent small shipments."

Then my friend added, "You know, you have a reputation as being pretty savvy in the field of physical distribution. I think you might be putting that reputation at risk by telling people your way of getting packages from Detroit to Kansas City is to transport them through Memphis." He had a point! Our customers were helping us to rethink how we described the service. We soon quit stressing the hub and concentrated on extolling the virtues of having our own fleet of planes and vans entirely dedicated to small packages.

We knew that most shipping departments were evaluated on cost per package shipped. Critical, time-sensitive shipments were typically sent "best way," which usually translated to Emery Airfreight or REA Express. We reasoned that speed, reliability, and convenience would be the driving elements in the decision to use our service. Clearly, we needed to reach potential decision makers beyond the normal freight traffic channels.

The field sales representatives worked to introduce new decision makers to our service, and occasionally used unconventional approaches to get the attention of prospective customers. When one sales rep was refused entrance without an appointment, he climbed a fire escape and knocked on the window of the prospective executive. When another rep failed to get a company president on the phone, he placed a collect person-to person call. The prospect, intrigued by the creative approach, saw him the next day. We reasoned that a unique new service with unmatched reliability warranted a dramatically different approach—and besides, we were getting desperate.

ASSEMBLING THE FIELD OPERATING GROUP

Fitz, Dennis, and others worked at a frantic pace to hire and train new employees for the new cities. By the time the research task force made its selection, they had only about two pressure-filled weeks to have fifteen new locations ready for the service. In several markets, they convinced their hotel to dedicate one of the unused phone extensions to the hiring process. The hotel operator would answer that extension with the phrase, "Federal Express, how may I help you?" That way, they were able to look for station facilities during the day and conduct hiring interviews in the evening.

Little Rock Airmotive rushed to modify more Falcons. The flight department worked to arrange airport approvals, contracted for ramp space and facilities, initiated airport familiarization flights, and prepared new flight schedules. We procured ground-handling equipment and delivery vehicles and completed numerous other tasks in the short time before startup. This time, we decided that our courier-salesmen should have uniforms with epaulets, stressing that our employees were part of an airline, so we jumped on that with off-the-shelf blue shirts, ties, and matching trousers.

Everyone was under pressure to meet the new deadline. There was no time for corporate politics, no time for petty turf conflicts, and no bureaucratic interference; just everyone knowing what needed to be done and working together toward the common goal. This was exhilarating! The team was coalescing into a wonderfully proficient and responsive organization.

THE OFFICIAL START

Finally, everything was in place and the big day—or more precisely, the big night—arrived. This time we made no fantastic or outrageous forecasts. We had learned an essential lesson—it was more important to be accurate than wildly optimistic. The new station managers and customer service agents received the pickup calls at the station. Couriers phoned the station after every stop, reported the number of packages picked up, and received information about the next scheduled pickup in their area. By maintaining this regular contact, each of the twenty-five stations had a reasonably accurate count of the packages by early evening. The stations phoned this information to Memphis headquarters, and before the arrival of the first plane, we knew within a few packages just what our volume would be.

"Fred reminded me that some new investors were going to be at the hub." Fitz recalls. "That got me onto the phone to everyone. We had people almost dragging packages out of the Emery driver's hands. The couriers and the station people in those days were really extraordinary."

The "official" beginning of Fred's imaginative concept on April 17, 1973, had taken just 22 months from the date of Federal Express's incorporation. Fred's good fortune and tenacious drive, along with about $25 million, had overcome seemingly impossible odds and fashioned a new business—the world's first and only airline specifically designed and operated solely for critical, time-sensitive small packages. The introduction of this brilliant new concept encompassed twenty-five cities, utilized a six-plane fleet, generated 185 package shipments, and left the company flat broke!

In the whole scheme of things, it was not an auspicious beginning. Our team was at first disappointed in the outcome, frustrated by our financial situation, and concerned about our families and our future. We could take some pride in the volume—30 times greater than the first night of the test run—but the results were still discouraging and even a little worrisome. Some of the uninitiated doubtlessly began polishing up their résumés. Others held going-out-of-business parties. Yet many of us felt if we could just hold on a little longer, Federal might succeed.

Rescue at the Edge
of a Precipice

The crunch of April 1973 was particularly severe and nearly overwhelmed our infant organization. To borrow Charles Dickens's famous opening in *A Tale of Two Cities*, "It was the best of times; it was the worst of times."

By now, the financial crisis grew more menacing every day. On several occasions, the company had no funds to pay its debts. Airports threatened to impound planes for nonpayment of landing fees, creditors threatened to stop supplying materials, lending banks threatened to ground the entire fleet until payments were made, and we stopped reimbursing management's expenses.

When our limited finances forced us to curtail our geographical expansion, we were in the troubling position of having more pilots than we needed for flight operations. However, we wanted to continue employing most of the qualified graduates from our flight school, knowing we would need them in the future. Our solution was to retrain the excess pilots for our customer sales staff or for station management until the package volumes grew to justify their return to flight operations.

"No man on earth will ever know what I went through in 1973 and 1974," Fred said, adding, "but it was nothing in comparison to Vietnam." The epic struggle for financial viability fell squarely on his broad shoulders. The management group assisted by keeping the company moving forward, but it was Fred's dedication, daring entrepreneurial spirit, and persuasive personality that carried us through those dark days.

FINANCIAL STRESS

The efforts to raise outside capital still weren't bearing fruit. We were getting favorable reactions from the venture capital community, and prospective investors agreed that Federal was an "interesting idea," but one by one, they elected to "pass at this time." It might have helped if the "trial" on March 12 had been successful or if the package volume in April had been more robust. The general condition of the economy also wasn't good. The financial markets were in turmoil; the Dow-Jones Industrial Average was steadily dropping from the 1,000 mark and, by the end of 1974, reached a low point of 578. Blue-chip stocks were selling at four to six times earnings. The prime rate was at 6.5 percent and would eventually increase to 12 percent by July 1974.

With expenses mounting, we were getting into deeper trouble financially. Things got so serious that one of our pilots used a personal credit card to pay for delinquent landing fees that would have prevented his departure from an outlying airport. Then, one of our couriers hocked his watch to buy fuel for his delivery van. Many of the couriers came in on weekends to wash and wax their vehicles. Wives often accompanied them to make familiarization runs through their territory. No one wanted to give up on our quest to keep moving forward.

Fred continued to obtain operating funds by using the Enterprise Company as the guarantor for loans from local banks, but everyone was getting nervous. To make matters worse, the third revision to the Falcon purchase agreement was due to expire before the end of May, and Pan Am was adamant that there would be no further extensions of the agreement. Either Federal Express would take the remaining Falcons by the agreed-on date, or Pan Am would retain the option money and commence selling the planes on the open market. It was truly the season of darkness.

Because I had done some consulting work with Purolator at about the time it purchased American Courier in 1967, I knew its key management. We were now so anxious for financial help that

Fred sent Fitz and me to explore the possibility of a joint venture with that company. The Purolator Courier group specialized in transporting bank documents and just could not see any benefit in joining our crazy scheme. They promptly turned down our proposal.

A LAST-MINUTE REPRIEVE

In desperation, Fred went to Brick Meers, assuring him that without the remaining Falcons, Federal Express could not possibly expand the network enough to sustain financial viability. It appeared to be the end of the road for Federal Express. Meers, in a last-ditch effort, arranged a meeting between Fred and Colonel Henry Crown of General Dynamics. Crown was sympathetic and seemed willing to help, but his financial adviser was in the hospital recovering from a hernia operation. He wanted to delay the decision until his key man returned to work.

Not one to be stymied, Brick phoned the hospital and got permission from the bedridden patient to make a presentation to him that afternoon. It took that kind of forceful dedication to keep the company afloat.

Three days before the expiration of the Pan Am option, the Chase Manhattan Bank, backed by a guarantee from General Dynamics, agreed to a four-month loan of $23.7 million. The company could now complete its option to take delivery of the remaining Falcons from Pan Am. Furthermore, the agreement allowed Federal Express to proceed immediately with the conversion of four more Falcons.

The General Dynamics guarantee kept us from financial collapse, but it came with a heavy price. Fred really had no other choice than to grant General Dynamics an option to acquire control of Federal Express. Though a bitter pill, it was the only way to avoid bankruptcy. When you are drowning, it is foolhardy to refuse a life preserver just because it's the wrong shape.

Immediately, a team from General Dynamics descended on Memphis to evaluate the cargo-handling systems and the Falcon's flight equipment. They looked at our budget forecasts, interviewed key management and operating personnel, scrutinized sales and marketing plans, and monitored the daily volume and customer service levels. In July, they reported that Federal Express had in fact achieved some excellent results for a startup. They complimented management for responding quickly to problems and finding new ways to improve operations, and concluded that the company would likely show a profit within a year. Despite the favorable report, the General Dynamics board of directors later decided they had enough problems of their own and did not exercise their option to purchase Federal Express.

However, several extremely beneficial things resulted from General Dynamics' involvement. The company did not just walk away and leave Federal Express unprotected; it continued to guarantee the Chase loan beyond the initial four-month commitment. The Falcons needed to complete the nationwide network were now in Little Rock, safely under our control. Just as important, General Dynamics' appraisal supported our concept and answered many of the technical questions raised by potential investors.

MOVING AHEAD

Within a month of the April startup, we added Boston, Wichita, and Baltimore to the network. The volume increased to four hundred packages daily. We were encouraged, but the banks and potential investors were apparently, as the good ol' boys from Memphis were fond of saying, still not convinced that this dog would hunt.

To generate new volume that might help persuade the reluctant investment community, Art launched a special direct-mail promotion called the Great Small-Package Air Race Sports Challenge. It was a fun piece featuring an old biplane on the front of the brochure, complete with goggled aviator and trailing scarf flapping in the wind. The promotion challenged the recipient to try beating Federal Express's service. The contestant was to send two packages, one with Federal Express and the other with any service with rates comparable to ours. If the participant found another service that beat Federal Express, we would buy the shipper two tickets to any sporting event of his choice. We did not have any takers, but several shippers responded that if we were that confident, they would begin using our service.

Bowing somewhat to outside pressure, and attempting to window-dress the company for the financial community, we decided to make a management change. I met with Mike off-site and said, "Look Mike, this is difficult for both of us, but after two startup opportunities, our volume is still anemic. We both know that you have done everything that could have been done under the circumstances, but we are going to reassign you to another position. Who do you think should take your place?" Mike thought for a moment and then suggested Fitz. I had some reservations, especially since Fitz had been with the company for only about 90 days, but Mike finally convinced me, and we went ahead with the first of many senior management shuffles. Fitz became the new senior vice president of sales and customer service.

Mike became senior vice president of corporate development, a new department that included Charles's operations research group. In fairness to Mike, we should have expected the rather dismal package volumes. Federal Express was a new, practically unknown company teetering on the edge of bankruptcy with a severely limited network and no ability to advertise its creative service to the potential shippers. We would remedy that in the future, but in the beginning, our growth was primarily by word of mouth, in effect a whisper campaign.

Early in June, we formalized our planning schedule for opening new cities, designing an eight-week preopening period of intensive activity following the selection of the next group of cities. Each department had a list of tasks to complete each week prior to the startup. We focused on continuing to expand the network, ignoring our inadequate funding.

Hundreds of suppliers continued to provide service and materials despite overdue invoices. The finance group, while husbanding our meager funds for the employee payroll and the most critical operating expenses, bore the brunt of abuse from disgruntled and irate suppliers. We hoped for the completion of the private placement very soon, but every time we thought we had it locked in, there was a delay. We operated on the dedication of our employees, the goodwill of our suppliers, and financial fumes.

By the end of June, the average volume had increased to more than 1,000 pieces per day. The shippers loved the service, and except for our dire financial situation, things were looking, if not more promising, at least less ominous. We were proving that rapid and consistently reliable service, even within a small network, would attract shippers of critical small packages and documents. This confirmation, combined with the General Dynamics report, ultimately convinced Charlie Lea of New Court Securities to help raise funds for Federal Express. This was a significant turning point.

We added Buffalo, Denver, Hartford, Louisville, and Minneapolis–St. Paul to the network the last week in July and Des Moines in August. Typical staffing at the new stations included two couriers, a customer service agent, and a station manager. The customer service agent (CSA) was a kind of short-order cook. The CSA did all the over-the-counter receiving, took all the telephone calls for the station, and acted as the dispatcher for pickups.

EVERYBODY PITCHES IN

The field service personnel developed close relationships with our customers, generating a small-package shipper group with intense loyalty to Federal Express. The couriers were always looking at the customer's collections of small packages and offering to take them if they were destined to one of our cities. Customers in turn cooperated, sorting packages to try to give us the ones that were destined for the areas we served.

Sometimes our couriers and salespeople got a little extreme in the items they accepted into the system. One evening Fitz and I were showing a prospective investor around the hub when we noticed an unusual shipment—a cage containing a sleeping bear and next to it a weasel in a smaller cage. We didn't dare check the weight of the strange shipment, but the investor asked where the bear was going. Fitz responded, "Wherever he wants to go." Around that same time, we had our first on-the-job injury; a few lab rats escaped from their shipping carton in flight, and the copilot got bit trying to get them back in their box.

Then we had the case of a microchip manufacturer who called to say we delivered an empty carton to his customer, explaining that the items were so tiny they might have spilled without our noticing. Later he called back to say we were not at fault—he had forgotten to put the chips in the carton. On another occasion, I noticed a large reel of plastic tubing at the Memphis station. "What are you doing with that?" I asked. The manager answered, "I'm cutting it into 50-pound lengths so it can be shipped."

One of the trickiest parts of the initial operation was handling calls for pickups late in the afternoon. In the beginning, the distance between customers was so great that it was almost impossible to make all the late pickups. The operating people soon learned to be creative and made deals with customers to leave the package somewhere that the courier could reach before the scheduled cutoff time. Dennis recalled, "Packages were deposited at bars, at friends' houses, and even underneath benches. Amazingly, people had such trust in Federal Express and our people that they were willing to do those kinds of things."

Station managers also made sales calls and even deliveries and pickups to maintain the service levels. Everyone became service oriented and did his or her part to expand the package volume and to assure that service commitments were met. Titles were meaningless when we needed special action. Everyone, including Fred, pitched in to help maintain the schedule and the service level.

Every person in the company knew that the leader and founder of Federal Express was Fred Smith, but few associates outside Memphis had actually met him. Like everyone else, to conserve funds, Fred rode the jump seat for some of his trips. One day, the plane was running a little late, and quick work was needed to make up for lost time. At the final destination city, Fred, as he did whenever he rode the jump seat, opened the Falcon door and immediately began handing down packages to the waiting station crew. As soon as the unloading was complete, Fred, sweat pouring from his brow, jumped down from the plane and stuck out his hand to introduce himself.

"Hi, I'm Fred Smith," he said to the ground crew member.

"Yeah, right, and I'm Elvis Presley," the skeptical ramp handler shot back. He just could not believe that the founder and president of Federal Express was riding the jump seat and unloading packages. Very few companies worked that way, and Fred took a lot of people by surprise. There was a wonderful informality and camaraderie in which everyone, irrespective of his or her position in the company, was committed to service excellence and did not allow titles to stand in the way of getting the job done.

18

Light at the End
of the Tunnel

The loan guarantee from General Dynamics raised our hopes and increased our spirits, but also increased the pressure to finalize the private placement. We continued to be in desperate financial trouble, particularly with our suppliers. The most demanding suppliers when it came to payments were the oil companies. Every Monday, they required Federal Express to pre-pay for the anticipated weekly usage of jet fuel. By mid-July our funds were so meager that on Friday we were down to about $5,000 in the checking account, while we needed $24,000 for the jet fuel payment. I was still commuting to Connecticut on the weekends and really did not know what was going to transpire on my return.

However, when I arrived back in Memphis on Monday morning, much to my surprise, the bank balance stood at nearly $32,000. I asked Fred where the funds had come from, and he responded, "The meeting with the General Dynamics board was a bust and I knew we needed money for Monday, so I took a plane to Las Vegas and won $27,000." I said, "You mean you took our last $5,000—how could you do that?" He shrugged his shoulders and said, "What difference did it make? Without the funds for the fuel companies, we couldn't have flown anyway." Fred's luck held again. It was not much but it came at a critical time and kept us in business for another week.

ENTER NEW COURT SECURITIES

We needed a lead dog, a strong member of the investment community that would step forward and give the other investors a sense of security. Fate sent us Charlie Lea, the executive vice president of New Court Securities.

George Montgomery, a partner in White, Weld, called Charlie in March to "come in and take a look at the project." "George," he replied, "I know just enough about airplanes to be dangerous." Montgomery sent White, Weld's private placement offering memo, which according to Charlie, "was an outrageous document. The financing and the terms were seriously a problem, but the idea for the business was interesting. It was at least worth a closer look."

Charlie, following his graduation from Cornell and a brief stop at W. R. Grace, spent 10 years working for Bessemer Securities Corporation, a personal holding company of the wealthy Phipps family. At the end of 1969, Charlie joined New Court, a firm owned by various banking affiliates of the Rothschild family, to manage its venture capital assets. The assets managed by New Court came from various U.S. institutions and pension funds.

Near the end of March, White, Weld arranged for Fred to meet with Charlie in New York at the New Court Securities offices. Charlie described his meeting with Fred this way: "We spent maybe an hour or so talking. Here was a young man who had just come out of Vietnam with a distinguished service record. He had put his own money in the company and was totally dedicated to it. Fred was the consummate entrepreneur type. There was no balance to him at the time, and he was going to spend every cent of a significant net worth to make Federal a success."

Impressed by Fred and the interesting concept, Charlie talked to some of his partners about the venture. They agreed Federal sounded interesting, so he decided to visit Memphis to assess the operation. Charlie and Rick Stowe, his counterpart from the venture capital side of New Court, were there for the April 17 inauguration of the expanded, twenty-five-city network.

"We waited up all night and watched the packages arrive. I got the drama of seeing the aircraft come in and got to see these decrepit Second World War facilities," Charlie recalls. "We went up to Fred's office, and there were books everywhere on the floor. It was apparent to me that he was trying to learn this business from scratch."

Charlie thought the operational side was well executed, and saw that we knew enough about airplanes to fly them, get them up in the air and back down again, and service them. However, he was concerned about the lack of seasoned management, uncomfortable with the cost of operations, and uncertain about the outcome of our struggle for market acceptance. He concluded that Federal was not an investment opportunity for New Court, so nothing happened at that time.

"Things were apparently getting pretty desperate for Fred," Charlie recalled. "He thought that Buck Remmell had deceived him and felt that Brick Meers was leading him down the garden path. When he first connected with White, Weld, he presumed they would take care of the finances, and that was a very naïve assumption. Fred did not understand that a best-efforts offering is not a guarantee to raise money."

A SECOND LOOK

By July we had been flying the service for a number of months and were tracking very close to the forecasts. After General Dynamics completed its report, its chief financial officer made a return visit to New Court. Charlie, encouraged by the assessment, began to think that this was something New Court could consider more seriously.

"The capital markets at that time were very difficult," Charlie recalls. "However, I began to see the possibility that in a short time, we could build a substantial company with revenues in excess of $100 million, something that Wall Street would find interesting. This was very important because investors must have some avenue to liquidity. It struck me that if we could get to the critical mass of the transaction, then we had a fair chance of succeeding."

Near the end of July, Fred and I flew to New York for a meeting with Charlie at the elegant New York Yacht Club. We met in the Model Room, impressively designed with glass cases containing models of the America's Cup challengers and defenders from

1851 to the present. On the walls are scaled half models of their hulls. Over dinner in this historic setting, we got the good news. New Court had decided to comanage the search for capital. Furthermore, Charlie indicated that Prudential Insurance and General Dynamics might also become investors in our private placement offering. By the end of the evening, we heard for the first time the most promising assessment uttered by any member of the Wall Street financial group: Charlie said, "It will not be immediate, it will be frustrating, and it will not be easy, but I am confident that we'll get the financing that Federal Express needs."

It was wonderful news, but I still had concerns. Venture capital companies were known for demanding a large chunk of the company ownership, promising contacts and guidance, but seldom delivering value. They were sometimes referred to as "vulture capitalists." If the startup succeeded, they took the credit and the lion's share of the reward. If it had difficulties, they often withdrew their support. The VC's approach was that out of ten investments, perhaps three would fail, three might break even, three would become somewhat profitable, and one would be a home run. It was a cold, calculated numbers game.

On the other hand, Charlie's approach appeared to be different. He seemed to be sensitive to the struggle we were having and, for the most part, complimentary of our progress. This red-haired Irishman possessed a sophisticated sense of humor and a mystical ability to make good things happen. I felt that having decided to become involved in the fund-raising, Charlie and New Court would make a sincere effort to advance the interests of Federal Express. They just might provide the outside support we desperately needed.

Charlie's confidence made me a little less apprehensive about our situation and more confident that with continued expansion of the network, we would succeed. I wanted to believe him. I was tiring of the weekly commute and frustrated with constantly being away from the family. Hopeful that bringing the family back together would alleviate some of the growing difficulties associated with absentee parenting, I decided to move everyone to Memphis. Once again, I was making the unforgivable mistake of unilaterally deciding what was best for my family, without giving them the opportunity to voice their opinions.

Charlie and his associate Rick Stowe started on our project soon after our meeting at the Yacht Club. New Court Securities was in a fee position as comanager of the venture capital deal with White, Weld. Charlie represented the venture capital side of New Court, and Rick the corporate finance side. New Court made the investment decision to put money into our company and to lead the whole transaction.

Charlie, Rick, and Brick invited interested parties to Memphis for a formal presentation by the General Dynamics project group and Federal Express management. Even with their strong efforts, however, the potential investors were first in the deal and then out and then back in again. "It was kind of like herding cats," Charlie commented. "We would package these guys up, send them down to Memphis, and they would all come back sold on the idea. Management was doing a splendid job of selling the potential investors, but as things dragged, on everyone became nervous. The fact is that in a deal like this the investors become followers only if there is a lead horse to follow. New Court Securities had to become the lead horse."

The management group was actually getting plenty of practice at selling the concept. The typical scenario included a get-acquainted dinner followed by a midnight rendezvous at the hub to watch the aircraft arrival and the package-sorting operations. The following day, managers from the various operating departments made presentations in our conference room and answered questions raised by the potential investors. We had such a practiced routine that we drew up a sheet with responses to the standard queries. At times, our staff would simply cite a number from the sheet with the comment, "Oh, yes, the answer to that question is number thirteen." The manager would then provide an explanation to answer the issue raised by the investor. It all sounded good, but in truth, number thirteen on the answer sheet read, "Obviously you have mistaken me for someone who can provide an understandable answer to your ridiculous question." It was a small, humorous way of keeping our sanity.

The ability to see the humor in the unfolding situations was one of our greatest strengths. No matter how frustrating or troubling the quest for funds became, no matter how dark the picture, our management team was able to keep events in their proper perspective. From a business standpoint, these were important, even serious matters, but from a personal point of view, they were not life or death issues.

HANGING ON THE EDGE

The banks that considered lending us the money to pay off our existing loans were trying to reach agreement on the prime rate add-on for accepting the risk of the venture. Meanwhile, the prime rate steadily rose from 7 percent in May to 10 percent in September 1973. These same institutions were also designing a complementary approach to get their fair share of warrants to purchase Federal Express stock at bargain prices when the company became successful. Chase Manhattan wanted to get out of the four-month bridge loan arranged by General Dynamics, even before the due date. Eventually, even some of the potential investors that had pledged their support grew concerned that Federal Express might not survive until the private placement closing.

The situation got so serious that one of the local banks, in a show of protecting its collateral, ordered us to ground the planes. Then, realizing that if Federal Express were unable to fly, all would be lost, the bank agreed to conduct its inspections of the "grounded" fleet twice each day—at mid-morning and early evening. This solution allowed us to depart early enough to make the evening pickups at the outlying cities and gave us time to return the planes to Memphis after the delivery runs. Frequently, the engines were still hot during the morning inspections, but the bank was ostensibly doing its duty to protect its security. It was a crazy way to run an airline.

By September the company was essentially bankrupt and by all counts should have closed its doors. We were running out of cash, vendors were threatening legal action to collect overdue bills, and on a few occasions, we had to ask employees to defer cashing their payroll checks for a few days. We would notify our employees that a date had been set for the expected closing of the private placement, only to have that closing postponed and another date set.

This was probably the most depressing and uncertain time in our young history. There just did not seem to be any way to overcome our financial predicament. In the midst of all this, Fitz and I planned a clambake to help raise spirits. We used a few of our connections to import lobster and clams from New England, shrimp from the Gulf, sourdough bread from San Francisco, Coors from Colorado, and bricks from a neighbor's construction site (Memphis has no rocks). It at least helped to take our minds off our problems for a short time.

From the very beginning, we kept our employees informed of the status of the company and its progress or lack of it. There was always a strong understanding that the employees had the right to know what was happening. While they might have found these reports frightening, our people adopted an air of invincibility. The unbridled passion and *purple-blood*, can-do attitude permeated all parts of Federal Express. Our employees got us through numerous setbacks and delays. Nearly all of our associates stayed the course and continued believing in the dream, adopting the Marine Corps motto, Semper Fi.

The August package count increased to 1,500 pieces a night. By the beginning of September, Fred, Charlie, and Brick finally won commitment for the full equity infusion from the group of private investors. The next challenge was to negotiate the bank loan so we could purchase the remainder of the Falcons.

Earlier, we had set our expansion plan to add cities on the West Coast beginning September 10, thereby providing a coast-to-coast network. In consideration of the continuing delays and our financial condition, we rescheduled that city expansion for the first week of October. The bickering over the loan agreement continued into mid-September. Fred and I jointly issued a memo to all employees, explaining the situation and noting that we expected increased funds to be available to us within 10 days:

> We would like to request from each of you that you do
> not cash or deposit your payroll check until next Monday,
> September 17, at the very earliest. . . . For those of you who
> can do so, it would be greatly appreciated that you hold
> these checks until we can announce to you that the inter-
> mediate funds have been received. . . . You may be assured

that your check, whether deposited today or next week, will be covered.

I suspect that some of them still retain that check as a badge of honor.

During September the daily package volume increased to more than 2,000 pieces—99 percent of the forecast for the month —adding credibility to the forecasting model developed by Art and his staff. The private placement still wasn't wrapped up, so we again decided to defer our West Coast expansion, this time to the end of October. Fred and I notified our employees of the deferral, optimistically stating, "The private placement will be in place by October 15." It wasn't; the banks were not finished with their negotiations.

Then, just when it appeared that things could not possibly get any worse, the Organization of Arab Petroleum Exporting Countries imposed the Arab Oil Embargo on the United States the third week of October. Prices for jet fuel, initially budgeted for $0.18 a gallon, began to approach $1.00 a gallon. Charlie's herd of cats was threatening to scatter once again. The banks were having an especially difficult time justifying their involvement in the credit agreement and demanded that the Enteprise Company make a significant additional investment in Federal Express. The embargo, coupled with an impending drop in the stock market, resulted in further delays. We were in a serious financial bind with no certain means of relief. It appeared as if the venture capitalists and credit institutions were in a feeding frenzy . . . and the victim was Federal Express.

As our package volume increased, we decided to move forward with our West Coast expansion plans, but with a reduced number of new cities. The last week in October, we began flying to Oakland, Los Angeles, Albuquerque, and Grand Rapids. The volume jumped to nearly 3,000 pieces daily, and the overall volume for October exceeded 50,000 pieces, slightly better than the forecast prepared for the General Dynamics report. The company systems appeared to be maturing and stabilizing even during a time of general economic chaos.

Despite the success of our growing network, the end of October marked a low point in our attitudes toward the financial community. At the same time, we knew that success was within our grasp if only the lending institutions completed their part of the deal. The fact that our operations were proving Fred's concept was a winner made the situation doubly discouraging.

OVER THE TOP

Finally, on November 13, 1973, the bloodletting ended and the first round of the private placement came to fruition with an equity infusion of $24.5 million and long-term bank loans of $27.5 million secured by a chattel mortgage on twenty-three Falcons. The other ten planes were security for the earlier loan from Commercial Credit Equipment Company. Some twenty-three institutional investors provided the equity capital. The long-term loans came primarily from the Chase Manhattan Bank, the First National Bank of Chicago, and a group of regional banks. It had been a difficult period, but Federal Express was over another of the many hurdles that lay on the road to success. We would face other difficulties in the future, but for now, as Fred and I declared to our anxious employees, "SUCCESS! We are launched." After months of anxiety and frustration, the 750 loyal, dedicated people of Federal Express could breathe a collective sigh of relief.

Charlie's decision to become involved, to think more seriously about aiding Federal Express, had been a turning point in the company's struggle. Charlie was quite simply the driving force that eventually made the private placement funding possible. Together, Charlie and Fred overcame obstacles that could easily have defeated lesser individuals.

The total funds of $52 million made this the largest venture capital private placement financing in the history of the United States up to that time. In the euphoria of the closing, we issued small but significantly important bonus checks to all employees with a personal note from Fred: "Rome wasn't built in a day. It might have been if Federal Express employees had been in charge." It was a victory of sorts for Fred and his dream for Federal Express, but it had come at a high cost to him personally and to the Enterprise Company; they no longer had outright control of the company. The outside investors and lenders were in charge.

Furthermore, the credit agreement called for the banks to withhold $5 million of the long-term loan. They would retain the funds until Federal Express complied with covenants contained in the ninety-page credit agreement. Those covenants required the company to become profitable ahead of the aggressive fiscal 1974 business plan prepared before the financing.

By the time the private placement was completed, the monthly revenues were already falling short of those projections. It was unrealistic to expect that the company could meet the covenant requirements. Before the ink was dry on the credit agreement, it was obvious that Federal Express would not receive the next infusion of $5 million. By the time the company paid off the previous creditors, very little remained for future operations, and a second round of financing appeared inevitable.

19

A Little Help from Our Friends

A s Thanksgiving 1973 approached, we tried to count our blessings. The mail runs were becoming routine, the Falcon modifications were progressing satisfactorily, and the priority package network now included thirty-eight cities stretching from Boston to Los Angeles and Miami to Minneapolis. Service levels stood at over 97 percent, and package volumes were steadily increasing. Still, we weren't out of the woods yet, not by a long shot.

Our anxious local lenders were repaid from the private placement funds, and replaced by equally apprehensive and even more rigid national institutions. The stringent covenants that allowed the banks to withhold $5 million of the "committed" funds meant that we would not breathe too easily. During the ensuing months, we frequently wondered if we were making any real progress on our quest to make Federal Express financially viable.

Following the closing, Charlie, Brick, Larry Lawrence, and Phil Greer joined the board of directors to represent the investors and banks. Charlie described the early board meetings this way: "The first board meeting was like fight nights at Starkey's. Representatives of every investor were lined up two deep around this huge table. They each had their own questions and their own agenda. It was like a free-for-all. It was virtually impossible to get anything done under those conditions."

This was not the typical venture capital deal. It was big relative to most venture capital deals at the time, and

111

each participant wanted a say in the operational aspects of the company. In order to bring some order to the chaos, we designated a committee of three to represent the interests of the investors and lenders—Larry Lawrence for the banks, Phil Greer for the investor group, and Charlie to head the committee. Gradually, after a meeting or two we got most of those who were not supposed to be there out of the room.

· Everyone knew that getting the first deal done was just the opening chapter in the search for financial viability. The package volume was steadily increasing but not rapidly enough to generate excess funds for the expanding operations. Everyone started working on a new round of financing. As early as 90 days after closing the first private placement, the investors and lenders met in Memphis to discuss the company's critical need for additional funds.

THE FUEL ALLOCATION CRISIS

The Arab Oil Embargo had resulted in skyrocketing prices for jet fuel, and President Richard Nixon had signed the Emergency Petroleum Allocation Act, which authorized allocation of and marketing controls on all petroleum products. Beginning in January 1974, airlines were to be allocated fuel based on a percentage of their 1972 consumption, which meant pretty close to no fuel for Federal Express.

The fuel allocation crisis sent everyone scurrying to Washington. The Department of the Interior was trying to administer the program through the sleepy Office of Oil and Gas. The allocation program was dumped in the agency's lap, and there were no forms or procedures to get fuel if you did not have a record of historical usage. Nat and Tuck went to the Office of Oil and Gas and got to know the secretary who was typing the forms. Tuck and Nat calculated the amount of fuel we needed and were the first in the hopper to apply for emergency relief.

"We had to be early," Nat recalled, "because we read the regulations and we knew that Federal Express's allocation was only going to be a few thousand gallons of jet fuel. We estimated the projected requirement for 1974 at about four million gallons."

The agency granted us an allocation of less than one million gallons. An official with the Office of Oil and Gas explained, "Everybody will experience some hardship and you are no different from anyone else." Tuck and Nat argued that in fact we *were* different because we were not in business in 1972, and so we were in a situation not even acknowledged in the regulation. The official responded, "Well, that is just tough luck."

Then, Fred went to Howard Baker, the second-term senator from Tennessee and asked him to set up a meeting with the director of the Office of Oil and Gas. Tuck and Nat, this time with Fred, returned to Oil and Gas to make the case for reconsideration of the initial decision. They began the meeting by explaining our unusual circumstances and the extremely important commercial and human value of Federal's specialized service.

The director and Fred then began reminiscing about people they had known and lost in Vietnam. "It was clear that the director, a navy admiral, was very impressed with Fred," Nat recalls. "As the meeting ended, the admiral said we had made a very persuasive case for the grant of emergency relief and that ours was a compelling story of both the emergency circumstances and a very clear public benefit."

Tuck and Nat went back to Nat's office and drafted a petition for reconsideration of the earlier action, not citing the meeting with the director but simply reiterating the arguments they had made previously. Approximately a week later, we received our allocation for 4.3 million gallons.

"It was just crazy," Tuck recalled. "The potential investors were concerned that we would not be able to get any fuel, but our quick action resulted in the welcome award—and it really was an award."

However, getting the allocation solved only half of the problem. The next challenge was to find a company that would sell us the fuel to meet the allocation. Federal Express came under the category of general aviation sales, and the fuel companies already had their hands full trying to allocate fuel among the passenger airlines. They did not want to add to the confusion by channeling fuel to our upstart organization. Fortunately, Charlie had a friend, his nephew's godfather and a former P-51 pilot, who was the head of all general aviation sales at Exxon. We got our supplier for the new allocation.

THE TEAMSTERS TAKE NOTICE

Our small but growing company was beginning to attract the attention of the Teamsters Union. Some of the trucking locals, particularly in St. Louis and Kansas City, began harassing our couriers. There were numerous incidents where trucks halted access to shipping docks or blocked alleyways leading from the delivery areas. Shippers were urged to stop using our service and told that we were losing packages and soon would be going out of business. On more than one occasion, couriers were forced to the curb and threatened. The Teamsters organization dismissed the activity as an unfortunate overreaction by a few local hotheads, but did nothing to end the intimidation. We counseled our couriers to remain calm while we called the police to remove the obstructions. The problem eventually disappeared when the national Teamster organization refused to support the local actions.

A CLOSER LOOK AT OUR
SERVICE OFFERINGS

In November the package volume continued to grow, but we had to admit that our revenue projections had been too optimistic. The sales force was up to strength numerically, but five of the largest seven cities in the network were well below projected levels. Our modest direct-mail and sales-lead solicitation programs were missing the mark.

At this point, we were offering three levels of service: Priority One, overnight before noon delivery; Second Day Air; and Courier Pak, the prepaid, flat-rate envelope for documents requiring next-day delivery. BFJ Advertising, an affiliate of AAPG, now led by Vince Fagan, evaluated the service offerings and recommended a new marketing and promotional strategy. The message for our premier service was clear: Get broader coverage, and the volume will naturally increase.

However, the Courier Pak service was a problem. The service was different from anything else in the market, and volumes were not growing as rapidly as expected. Vince pointed out that prepayment for the envelopes might be deterring sales of the product. Most important, he concluded that responsibility for the rapid and reliable movement of documents usually rested on the shoulders of secretaries and mailrooms. This simple and intuitive observation, that the shipping *decisions* for priority documents were generally not made on the shipping dock, would profoundly affect our promotional efforts.

Vince also noted that our Second Day Air service was not unique enough to support the effort required for shippers to separate those packages from those normally given to REA, freight forwarders, UPS, or the Post Office. Confident that the enormous deferred-package market would eventually and naturally open to Federal Express as the service network grew, Vince recommended against a major effort to promote that service, cautioning that to do so might detract from the orderly growth of the Priority One service.

Finally, Vince urged us to recognize the importance of the receiver in making the shipping decision. "No matter who pays for the service," Vince argued, "it is the shipper's customer that ultimately suffers directly from late or lost packages." In other words, Vince urged us to stress to the shippers that our premier service can help keep their customers happy. We later followed up on this recommendation by placing stickers intended for the consignees on the priority packages. For example, packages from Dallas carried the sticker THIS PACKAGE WAS IN DALLAS YESTERDAY.

Vince and his associates at BFJ then proceeded to develop a series of strategic programs and promotional pieces for both short-term and longer-term implementation. Of course, the BFJ recommendations would take some time to implement and even longer to make an impression on the market, and we still urgently needed to increase our package revenue. So, at the beginning of December, we introduced a new small-package service called *Economy Air*, an inexpensive alternative to the priority overnight or two-day service that moved on a space-available basis and provided delivery within three days at rates that compared favorably with UPS ground and REA services. We also embarked on an ambitious plan to add three or four new destinations each month during the second half of our fiscal year ending in May 1974.

During the holiday rush, the monthly package volume soared to nearly 100,000 pieces, but the increase was not without problems.

A hat distributor in Texas began shipping all the ten-gallon hats we could carry, each in its own carton. We were filling the plane all right, but the revenue from the hat shipper, based on the weight rather than the size, did not even pay for the fuel needed to transport the boxes to Memphis. Now we needed to add a dimension-based rate for bulky, lightweight packages. The hat shipper gave us another lesson in the finer points of the air express business.

As we neared the end of 1973, there was another round of musical chairs for the management group. Most significant, Art became the senior vice president for air operations, and Fitz assumed responsibility for marketing. My early questions about Fitz's capabilities had now vanished. Irby, still commuting from his home in Arkansas, decided not to relocate to Memphis. Some of the established, comfortable working relationships would be changing in the upper levels of the management group. However, change is a normal part of growth. As W. Edwards Deming is credited with saying, "It is not necessary to change. Survival is not mandatory."

20

Summoned to a
Special Meeting

ackage volume dropped off in January 1974, and we
were once again on the down slope of our emotional
roller coaster. In February the lending banks gave
formal notification that the company was not achieving the conditions set forth in the loan covenants and, as
expected, refused to release the final $5 million of their
loan commitment. Charlie, Brick, and Fred continued
working diligently to raise additional funds for the second round of the private placement, but conversion of
the remaining Falcons began to fall behind schedule
because the banks were withholding the hoped-for funds.

In February, volume was up again, and it looked as
if the number of shipments in March would shatter all
previous records. Again our optimism soared. Overall,
despite the emotional highs and lows, we were hopeful
that we were beginning to see the light at the end of the
tunnel.

Once again, our optimism turned out to be pre-
mature as the light began to assume the shape of an
oncoming train, this time involving our founder. At the
beginning of March, the Little Rock Union Bank notified the Enterprise Company that its guarantee of a one-
year $2 million loan was overdue. Among the Enterprise
board members, no one except Fred was even aware of
the loan.

Fred now revealed that a year earlier he had forged
documents indicating approval of a loan guarantee by
the Enterprise Company without consent of the other

board members, specifically his two sisters and Bobby Cox, the Enterprise secretary. Our respected leader admitted his culpability to the Federal Express board of directors and to the investors and lenders we were counting on to support the second round of the private placement financing.

While it is possible to understand that, under extreme pressure, Fred was acting to save Federal Express from almost certain bankruptcy, and even to empathize with what he did, it nevertheless appeared to be a serious breach of conduct.

ROUND TWO OF THE FINANCING

The investors and lenders had previously scheduled a meeting for March 12 in Chicago to discuss the final arrangements for the second financing. There were more than twenty institutions contributing to the private placement. To speed things along, they planned to form task force groups to study individual segments of the company so that all could complete their due diligence studies prior to the closing. At this critical juncture, it was important for Fred to attend the meeting.

This time, Fred was on the defense. He explained that in February 1973, he acted in response to a request from White, Weld to put additional equity in the company in order to heighten the interest of the private placement investors. Aware that our operating funds were exhausted and concerned about the possible financial collapse of the company, Fred agreed to provide the additional capital. In expectation of quickly securing private placement funds, he unilaterally committed the Enterprise Company to guarantee the loan.

According to Charlie, the person who seemed most distressed about the handling of the loan documents was Fred himself. Charlie recalled that some of the investors voiced concern, and the group discussed whether Fred should stay or be fired, but no one thought he was guilty of stealing. Most agreed that the company would not be hurt if he stayed.

The investors and lenders' primary concerns were that their investment in our struggling company was not meeting expectations. Some of the group blamed our shortfall on inexperienced management, but Charlie had a somewhat different opinion. Charlie had confidence in the management and knew that external problems such as the delay in closing the first round of financing, the fuel situation, the banks' refusal to release committed funds, and the holdup in converting planes were major factors contributing to the shortfall.

Knowing that Fred would now have to tell his story to a grand jury, several attendees expressed concern that Fred's legal problems could interfere with his ability to manage the company. Because the investors and lenders felt that Fred should have a diminished role in running the company, they decided to seek an older, experienced airline executive to replace Fred as chairman of the board of directors and chief executive officer of Federal Express.

Our founder and leader, though chastised, would retain his position as president of Federal Express and, from the viewpoint of the employees, would remain totally in charge of the company. This was a wise acknowledgement of the employees' dedication and loyalty to their leader. However, changes lay ahead that would shake the very foundations of Federal Express. Strange and bizarre happenings were occurring in our little world of high finance.

In an unusual show of cooperation, the investors and lenders completed their due diligence studies and worked out the details of the next financing in just one week. The second round of the venture capital private placement was finalized the third week of March 1974. It provided more than $6 million of additional equity and included new loans of over $5 million—a total of $11.5 million.

Fred and the Enterprise Company were treated harshly; they now held only a 19 percent voting share of the company. On the other hand, Federal Express had finally reached Fred's goal of borrowing enough money to make partners of the investors and banks. It was now important for the participants to protect their original investments.

Meanwhile, the volume levels continued to grow rapidly as new cities were added to the network coverage and the new Economy Air service caught the fancy of economy-minded shippers. The March package count was double that of January, and

April was 10 percent higher than March. We were beginning to fill the airplanes, but in truth, much of the growth was in the lower-priced services. Moreover, the small-package revenue still trailed the projections contained in the business plan, expenses were growing just as fast as revenue, and monthly losses were not declining.

One heartening part of our operations was the improving service levels. But then Fred straightened us out on that bit of smugness. The last week of April, he opened the executive committee meeting by observing, "Last week we delivered 50,000 packages and our service level reached 98 percent. That is far superior to our competition, but let me point out there still were about a thousand service failures, which very likely disappointed many of our cherished customers. That is entirely unacceptable! After this meeting, I want each of you to examine your operations, think about what you can do to improve service in your area, reassemble on Wednesday to coordinate your efforts, and prepare a presentation for me at our next meeting." We still had much work to do.

A NEW CHIEF FINANCIAL OFFICER

Charlie now turned his attention to other issues. Getting an experienced chief financial officer had been on Charlie's mind for some time; he considered it, as he explained, "the most important assignment that I gave myself. There were a variety of people doing the books, some of whom didn't really understand financial reporting, and the numbers just didn't make any sense."

By mid-April, Charlie located his financial candidate. "I found Pete Willmott through a good friend who was Pete's classmate at Williams College. Pete, then 37, was general manager of the bakery division of Continental Baking in Rye, New York.

His background was ideal for Federal Express. He had landed his first job in the corporate planning section of the finance department at American Airlines. Pete explained, "I spent most of the time working on capital expenditure decisions in the cargo area. We looked at whether we should buy freighters. I was down there trying to plan routes for these freighters and it was tough.

They would not let me out of my cubicle. It was point-to-point stuff and very difficult to design effective routes. That experience was terribly important for me later on when I was assessing Federal Express.

"I was invited to a meeting where about twenty people were running around trying to figure out how to collect the receivables," Pete recalls. It was a typical session of those early years, with people from all different departments contributing. Pete noted that the biggest problem was billing accuracy, and that was why it made sense to have representatives from several different departments at the meeting.

Pete thought Federal Express was an idea with real potential. He thought things were a little disorganized, but felt that he could help us out. His American Airlines experience allowed him to see the merit of the hub-and-spoke system and contributed to his optimism about our organization.

Pete told Fred he was interested, and Fred promised to send an offer. "I was at my home in Connecticut," Pete recalls, "when two guys showed up in a sports convertible, came up my driveway, and handed me this Federal Express package. It was the offer. That was a classic. So I looked over the offer and accepted it." He became our new senior vice president of finance the first week of May.

PUSHING THE COMPANY FORWARD

When Pete first arrived at Federal Express, the General Dynamics people who were overseeing the finance group departed. A day or two later, he notified the board that we were in default on our bank credit agreement. "Things were at first kind of a mess," Pete recalls. "Any day I went into work, I felt I was helping to push the company forward a little bit.

"I had a good feeling about the people," Pete recalls. "We just had to become organized. We did that by day-to-day communications, getting everybody focused on a few important things." Pete instituted standup meetings to coordinate things. Every morning at 8:00, all the finance group heads assembled in his office. Each one gave a brief report summarizing what he or she had worked on the day before and what was going to happen that day. It was a vital communication tool that, over time, produced a coordinated, productive, and cohesive department.

Our corporate offices were still located in the 1940s hangar, built long before central air conditioning was a routine amenity. Our offices, while superior to those in Little Rock, were rudimentary. Pete's daughter Sara came to work with him one Saturday. She took one look at his surroundings and wrote him a note: "Dad, be happy even in an office like this." "I framed that baby," Pete says, "and I have had it in my office wherever I have been ever since. I thought that was terrific."

Meetings to work out the pricing strategies for each of the various service offerings were frequent during the early years, and Pete labeled one of the participants "One-Way Stewart." He explained the nickname this way: "We typically started our pricing meetings on Saturday mornings with a roomful of people, but as the day went on, people had to leave. One person who always stayed was Stewart, an information systems analyst. Whenever we considered a new pricing idea, if Stewart didn't like it, he would cite the programming difficulty, and it wasn't going to happen. I started calling him One-Way Stewart because things had to be done his way; there was no compromise. That was the real life during the early part of my career at Federal Express."

Pete had responsibility in the beginning for the computer operations, which were a mess. The biggest part of the problem was that Burroughs either could not provide adequate support service or were not inclined to try. Perhaps they too were concerned about our chances for success or our financial condition. We had Burroughs equipment for one reason and one reason only—the company would extend us credit. IBM would not lease us any equipment because of our financial condition.

Then after church one day, Pete started talking with a friend who mentioned that his company was selling its data center to the bank. Pete said, "Wait a minute, you can't do that. We need that center." Pete called Fred, and within a week we negotiated the purchase of the data center. That was our first IBM equipment, and it became the base for many future improvements to our data-processing capabilities. Pete was able to organize the financial part of the company with accurate, reliable reports and forecasts that helped provide confidence to the investor group. Sometimes things work out for the best, even when least expected.

By the end of fiscal year 1974, package volume was exceeding 10,000 pieces a day and increasing at a compounding rate of 20 percent each quarter. The company was providing service to fifty-nine cities in an area stretching from Massachusetts to California.

Unfortunately, the company was losing about a million dollars a month, collections were slow, and we were in default on some of our interest payments.

PART IV

One for All and All for One
June 1974 to May 1978

21

A General in the Guerrilla Camp

red decided to take a vacation, his first since the founding of the company. Federal Express was recovering from its past turmoil, but Fred's problems seemed to be growing. He was feeling the frustration of the past few months; he was unquestionably exhausted from his continual efforts to keep the company afloat and concerned about the embarrassing events of the past few weeks.

Meanwhile, the search for a new board chairman was bearing fruit. While Fred was on his mid-May vacation, the investor selection committee decided they had found their candidate. When Fred got back from his trip, he was informed that the new chairman had already been hired. Fred was angry that the investors hired the candidate without seeking his opinion, yet he accepted the situation as inevitable.

The candidate was 59-year-old Howell M. Estes, Jr., who had been the youngest four-star general in the air force and had run the Military Airlift Command. Following his retirement from the military, he assumed the presidency of World Airways, a charter airline based in Oakland, California. Estes met the general criteria established by the banks: he was a "candidate older than Fred with broad management experience and a background in aviation."

The general assumed his new position as chairman and chief executive officer at the beginning of June. The culture clash was immediate. There was never a real introduction to the management group, and Estes had no concept of the organizational structure or the way we were accustomed to operating. Fred accepted Estes and, at least outwardly, treated the general in a respectful manner. In reality, however, very little changed with the arrival of the new executive officer. Fred kept leading the management group just as he had always done, and the senior officers continued following his leadership.

Within a few weeks, after commandeering Tuck to arrange a refund on the California license plates for his Mercedes, Estes told me to arrange private parking places for all of the senior officers. I responded, "General, I'm sorry, but we are just not accustomed to doing that around here." Estes, clearly unfamiliar with the nuances of running an organization composed of free-thinking civilians, shot back, "Well, we're going to do it."

"If you would like to have your own parking place," I respectfully responded, quickly realizing that he was after all our new chief executive, "we will put up a sign for you. As far as the rest of us are concerned, Mr. Smith does not want a private parking place, and I do not want a private parking place. The rest of the senior officers work for us, and they are not going to have private parking places."

The general got his sign and parking place, but under the circumstances, it was difficult to understand the mentality that placed personal conveniences above the performance of our struggling organization. Frankly, Estes was accustomed to being pampered as the privilege of rank, but our idea of how people needed to be treated was too egalitarian to adopt a rigid military structure. Fortunately, Estes did not appear to be overly interested in delving into the day-to-day operations and for the most part remained content to let Fred continue his leadership.

Estes played a role that we might look on with disdain, but he played it well. Estes gave credibility to the company at a time when some of the investors and banks had lost confidence in Fred. Charlie was able to take Estes into meetings, knowing that he could impress everyone. "This big, broad-shouldered front man, almost wearing all his medals, looked like something straight out of central casting," Charlie explained. "With his ever-present cigar and his military carriage, the general looked like Daddy Warbucks. He could sit there in meetings with investors and bankers, looking and acting very much like a seasoned chief executive and pull things off.

"Everybody played their role," Charlie commented. "Fred's credibility with the investors and bankers wasn't very good in those days. We were quite certain that Federal Express was going to need a third round of funding. I could not have taken Fred back to the investors and convinced them to put in another nickel, so the general served a useful purpose."

BUSINESS WEEK PREDICTS SUCCESS

Two weeks after Estes arrived, the June 15 issue of *Business Week* contained a full-page article titled "Federal Express Takes a Nose-dive." The provocative title, meant to attract reader attention, was somewhat misleading and not completely reflective of the article's content, but it was nonetheless disturbing. Estes was outraged, but unable to persuade the magazine to print a retraction. Actually, some parts of the article were quite complimentary: "Customers generally agree that the promises of overnight delivery have been kept." The article also declared, "The bright spot at Federal Express is that it is living up to the promise of overnight delivery anywhere in its system. Federal Express has been able to maintain that record because, unlike Air Express, which depends upon commercial airline schedules, it makes its pickups in 61 cities and flies all of the parcels to Memphis."

The article continued, "The Company is growing at a rate faster than its management can adequately handle. In December, it was hauling about 5,000 packages per day. But by May, its daily volume was up to 11,000 packages. It is still compressing a normal three-year growth period into less than one year." Other parts of the article described, accurately, the ongoing financial difficulties as well as the operational and management changes explained in this book. The article concluded with the following appraisal from an investor: "They'll probably make it, but it'll be a tightrope situation for the next few months."

We prepared a memo to our employees with information they could use to answer customer questions about the article. With the exception of the misleading title, the article probably had no negative influence on Federal Express or the relationship with our customers.

In fact, the July package volume was well above the June level, and the August level exceeded the July level despite a substantial increase in rates. Pete convinced us that our customers would consider the increase an indication of our strength. In other words, they could trust Federal Express to be their priority small-package carrier of choice long into the future.

THE GENERAL'S REGRESSIVE APPROACH

During this period of dramatic growth, Estes started groping for ways to improve our bottom line. His approach was to look for cost-cutting opportunities. Distancing himself from day-to-day operations, he did not seem to grasp management's rationale for expanding the network. Our approach to making the company profitable was to add more cities while striving to increase customer awareness. We could have reduced expenses and taken a less aggressive approach, but there simply were not enough cost-cutting opportunities to make Federal Express profitable. In the end, there would not have been a company.

Estes commissioned a study to determine the cost to operate each of the cities in the network. The costs for each city were calculated by combining the facility operating expenses with the allocated flight cost based on the distance from Memphis, and adding a percentage for overhead expenses. Of course, by allocating flight expenses on the basis of the distance from the hub and compounding the factor by adding the overhead on a percentage basis, the cities at the far corners of the network looked as if they were the most expensive to operate.

Based on this convoluted analysis, Estes recommended closing the "high cost" cities at the ends of the service network—cities like Los Angeles, San Francisco, Seattle, Miami, and Boston. It was impossible to take that kind of recommendation seriously, so we just kept moving ahead, adding cities with confidence that the only road to profitability was to complete the network recommended in the original consulting studies. Commenting on the relationship between Estes and the senior officers, Fred noted, "It was like General Eisenhower attempting to lead Ho Chi Minh's guerrillas."

ROUNDING OUT THE SENIOR MANAGEMENT STAFF

September brought further changes to the senior management staff. Jim Riedmeyer, the former general manager of Southwest Airmotive Company in Dallas and a consultant to Federal Express on engine overhauls and other maintenance programs, yielded to Fred's enthusiastic salesmanship and joined the company as the senior vice president of maintenance and engineering at the beginning of the month.

One of my fondest memories of Jim took place during his first Saturday-morning executive committee meeting. About an hour into the meeting, while we were still waiting for Fred to arrive, Jim's secretary entered and placed a glass of orange juice and two small airline bottles of vodka on the table in front of him. That was his way of expressing his feelings about the need to meet on Saturdays. We knew immediately that he was going to fit in with the group.

In the beginning, I was a real neophyte on the internal workings of aircraft. Jim took special delight in showing me around the maintenance hangar and testing my knowledge of parts for the Falcons. By the time Jim joined our staff, I knew more about the planes, but he was always able to find a part to stump me. One turned out to be a small but important component of the jet engine. "I just wanted you to be ready for my budget plan," Jim explained. "We have two of those on each plane and they wear out. Their replacements cost $25,000 a pop."

Jim was uncompromising in his quest for safety and redundant backup systems on our fleet. He likened our planes to a space capsule that formed the life support system for our pilots and protected the public on the ground. His insistence on quality components, engineering improvements, and regular advanced training for our mechanics produced a safety record and level of dispatch reliability that were among the best in the industry.

Vince and Tucker, bowing to what might have been threats from Fred to forgo payment of their consulting services, decided to close the last vestiges of AAPG and BFJ Advertising to join the senior management group in Memphis. Vince, then 37, became our marketing senior vice president.

Tucker, 34 and a former navy carrier pilot, was hired as the senior vice president of industrial relations. The irreverent son of a minister, Tucker had been one year behind Fred at Yale. He was bright and exuberant and operated like a whirlwind. Charlie also had known Tucker prior to Federal Express. It seemed as if, in every case, either a special relationship from the past or an unknown force was at work building the original management group. Whatever the reasons, with the arrival of Jim, Vince, and Tucker, the executive management group that was to take Federal Express to profitability and beyond was complete.

Tucker, remembering his early days, said, "There was a lot of spirit, a lot of hard work, and a lot of macho fighter pilot psychology. We worked hard and we played hard. We were losing money, but that just seemed to motivate everyone. We were determined to make Federal work. We would challenge the establishment, provide a level of service never before attainable in the transportation industry, and create a whole new approach to the way business functioned."

Tucker once referred to our regular weekly executive committee meetings as "verbal fistfights." That description may have been a little strong, but heated discussions certainly occurred over many issues concerning upcoming activities and plans for the future. Fred was constantly the forward thinker and frequently encouraged these lively debates by proposing extreme concepts that often seemed far beyond the capability of our embryonic state of development. On one of these occasions, Fitz, in the descriptive visual language he favored, leaned over and said, "If Fred tells you a chicken can pull a freight train, your job is to hook 'em up."

The meetings were animated with a spirited exchange of opinions, but once the debate ended, often with Fred's prodding or intervention, and a decision was reached, each of us threw his full support behind it. The lively discussions, mutual respect, and camaraderie of the senior management resulted in a cohesive, well-conceived focus for the company.

Fred had an interesting way of checking on the corporate communication system in those early days. When an agreed-on action needed to be known by every employee in the company, he directed executive management to make certain the information was personally disseminated through the upcoming management and supervisory staff meetings. One week after the executive committee gathering, Fred would call one of the first-line employees, such as a mechanic, a customer service agent, or a courier. He checked to make certain the associate at the other end of the line knew about the decision made at the previous executive committee meeting. The process worked and was effective in an era before sophisticated electronic communications became a part of the Federal Express network.

The senior management structure at this point was composed of two interrelated groups. The staff division, which report directly to Fred, included Legal and Regulatory (Tuck Morse), Finance and Administration (Pete Willmott), Industrial Relations (Tucker Taylor), Marketing (Vince Fagan), and Critical Parts Supply (Mike Basch). The operating division, for which I was responsible, included Maintenance and Engineering (Jim Riedmeyer), Field Sales and Service (Mike Fitzgerald), Air Operations (Art Bass), and Operations Planning (Charles Brandon).

While we had a formal management chart, we all saw our roles as flexible and at times interchangeable. Organizational silos just did not exist. The senior management group served as the catalyst for guiding the company through this critical growth period and set the tone for the enthusiastic and unwavering commitment to success.

It was, however, the dedication to excellence exhibited by the managers, supervisors, and first-line operators that made Federal Express especially unique. The loyalty of the couriers, customer service agents, mechanics, pilots, ground crews, and technical support staff pulled the company through many of the difficult times. Josiah Royce, in the *Philosophy of Loyalty*, describes loyalty as "the willing and thoroughgoing devotion to a cause that unifies many human lives in one." Our people were true examples of that brand of loyalty.

22

Fund-Raising—Round Three

It was time to begin planning for a third round of financing. Charlie and Rick Stowe began visiting other venture capital groups in the hope of attracting new investors by midsummer, but they found no takers. Charlie explained, "It was a tough time generally in the financial community. This was 1974 and the capital markets were in the tank." Charlie realized he needed another source of funds for the third financing.

At his urging, we sent our best, most eloquent and personable ambassador to Paris for a face-to-face meeting with the Rothschild family. Art had a natural ability to charm our harshest critics. Over lunch with Baron Guy de Rothschild, his son David, and nephew Nathaniel at their Paris office, Art explained the mechanics supporting the optimistic growth projections for the company: each new city opening created shipping opportunities from and to every city already in operation. It was a straight numbers game at this point. The baron was impressed with Art's elegant presentation and decided that the bank would participate if his son and nephew invested their own money, as well. To our relief, they agreed.

This coup was a tremendous help, but the Rothschilds were the only new investors. "We were able to piece together that last round by convincing the banks to renew their loans and to defer principal and interest payments for a period of time," Charlie recalls. "We finally explained to the banks that without their cooperation, planes would sit on the ground in Memphis and draw flies. We needed $9 million. I could raise only $3 million.

So the banks had to provide the rest. Having to deal with the banks and everything else that was going on at this time was a bloody nightmare.

"The next thing was to get positive cash flow so we could begin paying bills on a current basis and pay back some of the borrowings from the bank," Charlie added. "So by bits and pieces we gradually got all these things put together, and eventually we had an operation. It was quite amazing." At that point, Charlie wrote a letter to Fred:

> We have just shot our wads between banks, investors, and oil companies; the next money that comes into this company has to come from the customers. The internal issues of the company will become totally different after that. If you are as successful in developing Federal Express as you were in convincing half of the venture capitalists in America, we will all be very happy.

Charlie's prediction at that New York Yacht Club dinner some 14 months earlier had finally come home. It had not been immediate, it had absolutely been frustrating, and it had certainly not been easy, but we got the funding needed to complete our network, and at last were on our way.

NEW CORPORATE OFFICES

September 1974 also witnessed the opening of our new corporate offices, a three-story building connecting Hangars 6 and 7. The management group was elated about the new facility. I was able to move out of the tiny windowless closet that had served as my office. Everyone got bright, cheery offices, our new conference room actually had chairs and a table, and best of all, our beleaguered leader finally had an office that did not have a hole in the floor.

Earlier, as Ted Weise watched over the completion of the new offices, Estes called and asked to review the plans. Ted grabbed the plans and headed for the general's office, where he started explaining the plans for the first floor, but Estes interrupted saying, "Where is my office?"

Ted showed him the plans for the executive floor, pointing out Fred's office and the office planned for him. Estes said, "Well, it looks like Fred's office is paneled. That is now *my* office." Afterward, Fred was philosophical saying, "Ted, don't worry about it. Give him what he wants." Fred never said anything more than that. Estes moved into the office, cigar and all.

GENERALS NEVER MAKE MISTAKES

No one—not Fred, not our management group, not the investors, not the banks—wanted to go through another fund-raising exercise. We were more determined than ever to put that unpleasant task behind us and generate at least a positive cash flow, if not downright profitability. We developed a major program to augment our direct sales teams. Senior managers began contacting large shippers, prospective customers, suppliers, and anyone else who would listen to us.

On one of these occasions, I arranged for a sales presentation on a major air force facility to explain the Federal Express program and solicit business from the military. I made my presentation to the commanding general of the facility, his aide, and several other air force personnel. I learned two interesting facts during that briefing. First, during my presentation I thought I had cleverly worked around to noting that our new chairman was a retired four-star air force general. The commanding general, who had been listening intently to the story, suddenly interrupted: "Oh, yes, we are very familiar with your new addition. However, let me give you a word of advice before you visit other military installations. You do not get to be the youngest four-star general in the air force without stepping on an awful lot of toes and making a few enemies." Enough said. I took note of the general's advice and did not mention our new arrival thereafter.

I continued to extol the virtues of our service and could see from the questions that there was at least some interest in using us for high-priority emergency shipments of parts and supplies. It seemed that we could at least save the air force some expenses.

Federal Express was, after all, cheaper than sending one of their fighter jets on such an errand. (Fred later reminded me that my logic was flawed. I was expecting that people trained to make war would make decisions based strictly on cost efficiency.)

As my presentation was nearing its conclusion, the general thanked me for the information, but said that the facility operated seven days a week and would need to have deliveries made on the weekends as well. We did not have weekend deliveries at that time. The aide leaned over and whispered something to the general, who then said to me, "We would like to take a break. Excuse us for a few minutes."

When they returned, the general, who had been quite cordial up to now, looked at me more seriously and said, "I have just been informed by my aide that if you attempted to deliver a package to this post on the weekend, there would be no one here to receive the shipment." Then with a broad smile, he added, "Here is another thing for you to keep in mind . . . this little piece of inaccurate information stays in this room. Remember, generals never make mistakes." Then we all had a hearty laugh: after the general assured everyone that his directive was a joke, humor was acceptable and appropriate. As a former navy enlisted man, I received two very good lessons in higher-echelon military etiquette.

DIGGING FOR GOLD IN NEW YORK

At one of those early "verbal fistfight" meetings, an investor representative suggested discontinuing service to the cities with the highest number of freight forwarders. Now, this was a challenge that Vince welcomed. "Oh, and why do you feel that way?" Vince asked.

"Because there is just too much competition," was the answer. "We have researched five of the major cities in your network, and there are dozens of well-established freight forwarders in each of the locations. You should be concentrating on cities with less competition. When the elephants are running, the mice need to get out of the way, and Federal Express is a mouse compared to those large freight forwarders."

Vince, not one to be intimidated by a challenge to his marketing knowledge, replied, "Let me tell you why those locations have dozens of freight forwarders. It is because that is where the business is! That is why Federal Express needs to be there. In 1849, you probably would have been digging for gold in New York because no one else was searching there."

THE CHALLENGE OF SUCCESS

Traditionally, one of the better volume months for many transportation companies is October, when summer vacations are over and businesses begin to build inventory for the upcoming holiday season. This October, however, surpassed all expectations at Federal Express. The Teamsters Union was threatening a strike at UPS, and shippers began looking for alternative carriers. Our volume peaked at over 300,000 packages that month and was near that level in November when the strike threat became a reality. Suddenly, we were straining our ability to handle the volume surge.

While we began to struggle with the limited space on the Falcons, we started looking for ways to increase the number of units we could transport. We considered various alternatives for accomplishing this goal and settled on an increase in the number of Courier Paks. At that time, customers still had to prepay for their Courier Paks, and Pete worried that prepayment was inhibiting the growth of that product. Fagan, who had made that same argument earlier, now favored keeping the prepaid service as a means of increasing our cash flow. It was a strange reversal of roles.

"In the new administration building I had an office right next to Vince," Pete recalled, "and I frequently drove him to work too. We would get into some unbelievable discussions, but I think the Courier Pak debate was the strangest one." Pete and Vince's discussions frequently carried over to the nearby Sawmill restaurant, where after work they and other members of the management group often congregated to continue hammering out alternative solutions and approaches to upcoming challenges and opportunities. Egos were seldom involved, and more important, the process worked. Eventually Vince agreed with Pete, and our Courier Pak service really started to take off.

After the change, the Courier Pak became easy to use. Customers found it convenient to have a large supply of Courier Paks on hand and began using them to send materials between their own and other companies' offices. That was critical for another reason: it also kept our couriers entering the front offices, reinforcing their image with the service-minded decision makers. There were fits and starts and some things required modifications in the beginning, but Federal Express's concept was so sound that as long as we continued listening to our customers, they told us what our business needed to be.

Customers began using our service for so many routine tasks that some labeled us "Federal Excess." One secretary, for example, used Courier Paks for daily reports to the business office across the street so she could avoid the catcalls of construction workers. Manhattan courier companies reduced their expenses by using our Courier Paks for documents to Long Island. Branch managers frequently ignored corporate office dictates to reduce their use of Federal, arguing that our speed and reliability had become a necessary part of their business.

The U.S. Postal Service was concerned about the Courier Pak service, and as we became more visible, it sent postal inspectors into the hub. They actually opened the Courier Paks and examined the contents; they had the legal right to do so. The Post Office eventually insisted that we had to tell our customers to weigh the correspondence in each Courier Pak and determine the applicable postage. In fact, it even took the position that the customer should affix, not first-class postage, but the premium for the best service the Post Office then offered. We put a notice on the envelope directing customers to put "appropriate" postage on their letter correspondence. The Post Office accepted that statement, knowing that since the shippers put postage on the "letter" inside the envelope, Federal Express had no way of assuring compliance with the postal requirements. Eventually, the Post Office's position changed and the requirement simply vanished.

23

America, You've Got a New Airline

In December 1974, after the end of the UPS strike, volumes dropped back to a more normal level but remained more than double the level of the previous December. We added fifteen new cities to the network during the second half of the year. The rapid pace of expansion and the explosive growth of the volume kept everyone running at maximum effort. The days were long, the weekends short, and pressure was intense. Nevertheless, we were meeting the challenge and we all loved the excitement! The financial picture was even beginning to look better: December was the first month that cash income was greater than expenses.

We were now concerned that our volume might exceed the capacity of the Falcon fleet, so we decided to discontinue the Economy Air service. We began to anticipate a time when we would need to cancel the mail contracts and place those planes in the small-package service.

Then another surprise: The package volume for the first few months of 1975—in fact, for the rest of the fiscal year—remained stubbornly flat. However, since we attained the volumes without Economy Air packages, the revenue was elevated, and cash receipts continued to run about equal to disbursements. We were all breathing a little easier and even managed to feel a little bit smug about our success. We were finally reaching the initial point of financial stability and were confident that real profits were just around the corner.

BUSINESS-TO-BUSINESS TELEVISION ADS

Despite our jubilation over the package numbers and the financial situation, Vince, mindful of the relative stagnation in the package volume and ever critical of the direct sales effort, lobbied for an expanded advertising program incorporating radio and television commercials in addition to print media. Business-to-business television advertising was at the time a novel, unproven concept, but Vince was convinced that television was a perfect medium for Federal Express.

Vince proposed a trial program composed of thirty-two cities with comparable package potential, half to receive television commercials aimed at the shipping public and the other half to remain on the direct sales program. Funds were scarce, but in a show of selflessness, several department heads offered to reduce their already slim budgets to support the project.

Several ad agencies made presentations to the senior executives. One agency showed up with storyboards that had been shipped ahead via Emery Air Freight. We decided they were not the right agency for us. We ultimately settled on Ally and Gargano Advertising for our first try at television.

Carl Ally, the president and cofounder of the agency, was a brash, hard-hitting advertising executive. Ally was the person responsible for winning a change in television rules against mentioning the competition in commercials. He also refused to design advertising promotions for cigarette companies. He was not afraid to take on corporate underdogs, and he enjoyed handling accounts that were new or troubled. Carl Ally was perfect for our upstart company.

Other transportation companies were handling small packages, but as the consulting studies had discovered, those companies were not able to provide reliable overnight service. UPS, founded as a private messenger and delivery service in 1907, and the model for many of our operating systems, had a reputation for great efficiency among its regular customers, but was insensitive to the needs of infrequent, on-call shippers. UPS normally scheduled a pickup the day following a request for service. Tracing a lost shipment could take up to a month. UPS's priority package service, Blue Label, flew in the cargo holds of regularly scheduled airlines and was not available to every state until 1978. UPS did not enter the overnight air delivery business with its fleet of chartered aircraft until 1982. REA Express offered a priority airfreight service but also depended on the scheduled airlines for interstate transportation.

Hundreds of airfreight forwarders throughout the country offered service for small packages. Emery Air Freight, founded in 1946, was the largest and perhaps the most successful of these companies, but like the others, it relied on scheduled airlines and could not provide consistent reliable overnight service, especially to smaller communities. John Emery complained that flight reductions were eroding the quality of airfreight to a two- or three-day service. Emery did not launch its own fleet of leased planes until 1976, and even then operated only a few Cessna Citations, primarily for its overnight letter service using a hub in Smyrna, Tennessee. Emery added planes for its freight service in 1981 when it opened a new hub in Dayton, Ohio.

The scheduled airlines faced the same problems as the airfreight forwarders: interline transfers at major hubs, poor service to small communities, lack of origin-to-destination control, and difficult communications with Air Cargo, Inc., their jointly owned surface carrier. Even the U.S. Postal Service's Parcel Post suffered from these problems.

Federal Express until about 1980 was the only company that could realistically guarantee nationwide overnight service. The television commercials designed by Vince and Ally and Gargano were structured to introduce the Federal Express concept to the shipping public and to highlight our ability to maintain control of the package from pickup to delivery. The first commercial opened with a plane heading directly at the viewer, landing lights beaming out of a slightly overcast twilight sky:

America, you've got a new airline, the first major airline in over 30 years.

No first class, no meals, no movies—in fact, no passengers, just packages. Small important shipments that have to get where they're going overnight, and up to now have had to fly at the mercy of the passenger airlines.

Not anymore.

FEDERAL EXPRESS—A WHOLE NEW AIRLINE FOR PACKAGES ONLY.

The second commercial got more specific about the freight forwarder competition and the inherent advantages of Federal Express:

The trouble with airfreight forwarders is, they don't know how to fly, so they have to depend on someone who does. And the more people involved in shipping a package, the less chance of it getting there the next day.

Which is why when we decided to go into the air express business, we didn't just go out and get a fleet of trucks.

We bought a fleet of planes.

FEDERAL EXPRESS—WE THINK ANYBODY IN THE AIR EXPRESS BUSINESS OUGHT TO BE ABLE TO FLY.

Vince's trial program, despite a very limited, budget was a success. He demonstrated the power of business-to-business television advertising and thus began the conceptual approach to promoting our unique service that propelled Federal Express into the forefront of the priority small-package transportation industry.

TESTING OUR SERVICE

Confident in our ability to provide a more reliable overnight service than any of our competitors, Vince hired Opinion Research Corporation to conduct a test pitting Federal Express against Emery Air Freight, Airborne, and REA Express. In April 1975 the independent firm sent identical packages between forty-seven city pairs using both Federal Express and the competing services. The results clearly showed the superiority of the Federal Express system. Emery, the best of the three competitors (and generally considered to be "the best in the business"), delivered only 42 percent of its packages the next day. Federal Express's deliveries were 93 percent on time. Furthermore, the study concluded that Federal Express's tracing capability was superior to the others and our total charges were lower than the competition's.

We presented the test results in a brochure mailed to several thousand potential customers and published the results in numerous print advertisements. Ally and Gargano produced a TV commercial citing the test data and showing stacks of packages representing the comparative service level. The production closed with the line, "I guess that makes Federal Express twice as good as the best in the business!"

Emery threatened a lawsuit but eventually decided that our case was too strong. It was a wise decision: the publicity surrounding a court case would have been even more beneficial for Federal Express than the television advertising. The ad was a bold, direct response to Emery's claim that its service was "a dollar less and an hour faster" than its competition.

Having reached a state of relative comfort with our financial condition, Fred had become increasingly critical of the facilities we leased for the outlying city stations and at airports. In Manhattan, for example, our space was so small that on rainy mornings, the incoming package sort took place under the 38th Street overpass. To make matters worse, we parked our vans outside overnight where meter maids from the nearby school began their day by ticketing our illegally parked vehicles. At many of the larger airports, we could load and unload our planes only at an isolated part of the field; ramp agents had to phone Memphis to report aircraft departure times.

Fred and I discussed the issues and decided that I would lead a field reorganization team with responsibility for correcting the conditions. This special project team, assembled to focus top-level attention on a specific issue for a limited duration, was a typical means for handling areas of concern in the early years. We prepared a draft memo outlining the team's composition and responsibilities for distribution the day after our upcoming board meeting. Before I could begin, we were hit with yet another crisis.

24

A Threatened Resignation

It was Wednesday evening, February 26, 1975—little more than three years after my first meeting with Fred. I was reading over material for the next day's meeting of the board of directors. It was an uncommon pleasure to have an evening free of the social dinner and obligatory midnight hub tour for the steady stream of interested visitors and potential investors. The outside directors were doubtless already in town, perhaps having their traditional pre–board meeting discussions. There was, after all, much to discuss and for the board to be apprehensive about.

About 10:00 my phone rang. I was surprised to hear the abrupt voice of our leader: "Roger, this is Fred Smith."

"Hi, Fred," I responded. "What's up?"

"I just wanted to let you know before our board meeting that I am resigning from the company tomorrow."

"What? You can't be serious."

"I am dead serious," he stressed, "and I have just finished writing my letter of resignation that I'll submit to the board tomorrow."

I knew that Fred had been under a tremendous amount of pressure. I could hear the tension in his voice. The current situation was depressing for him, but I also knew that his continued guidance was crucial to the future success of the company.

"But why," I asked, "when you are just on the brink of realizing your dream for Federal Express? Why now?"

"Well, I've decided it's best for me and best for the company. I've made up my mind and that's the end of it. I'll see you in the morning."

"Wait a minute, Fred. Where are you right now?"

"I'm in my office and getting ready to leave in a few minutes."

"Will you stay there a little longer until I can get there so we can talk about this?" I suggested. "This decision affects all of us, and I would like a few more answers before tomorrow's board meeting."

"I have made up my mind and you are not going to change it, but OK, I'll stay until you get here." Then silence on the line. He had hung up.

Why was this happening when we were just on the threshold of almost certain success and financial sustainability? Why had Fred chosen this moment to abandon the concept that he had forged into a meaningful, reliable service to thousands of customers? He was the respected leader of our employees, and to the outside world, he *was* Federal Express.

What was going on here? Sure, he had personal problems, but the Fred Smith I had come to know was not one to back away from troubling situations. Somehow, I had to at least try to change his mind. There was an opening, an outside chance, if we could talk. I needed additional support and fast.

I dialed Fitz, always one of the most persuasive members of our management team. He concurred that Fred's resignation would have a potentially devastating effect on our fellow employees and possibly on the company. "I'll pick you up in 10 minutes," Fitz said.

We parked in the lot adjacent to Hangar 7 at the Memphis airport, the aging World War II building that had served as our temporary executive offices. Fitz and I took the elevator to the third floor of the new administrative building and walked down the short corridor, past the conference room where the directors would be meeting the next morning, and into Fred's office.

Fred looked terrible; the pressures of the past few months showed on his face and were apparently affecting him in many other ways. Fitz and I began discussing the situation with him, trying desperately to find out the real reasons behind his decision to resign. First in an irritated fashion, then more thoughtfully, he explained all of the things that had contributed to his decision. Some we already knew about, others were a surprise, but overall, we were gradually coming to understand his state of mind.

Fred was tired, worn down by the pressures of the past few months, and depressed by recent events, especially the grand jury investigation. His sisters were angry about the undisclosed Enterprise loan guarantee, and his private life was in shambles. He was disturbed that Estes had been hired without his involvement, and to make matters worse, the outside directors representing the banks and investors had apparently lost confidence in him.

By now it was early morning and activity was increasing around the hub. A few pilots, seeing the lights on in Fred's office, drifted up to chat, so we decided to retreat to a more private area in Hangar 7. Fitz and I began to steer the conversation away from Fred's depression and toward the important things that he had accomplished over the past few years.

Fred had led the company through our troubled times without complaint and had seldom shared his burdens with the management group. He was never a very open person, preferring instead to keep his emotions behind an impenetrable wall, but gradually he began to relax. Now, for the first time, he began to open up and share his personal feelings. As he sensed our trust and goodwill, his outlook gradually improved. Suddenly he said, "Man, I could really go for a beer. What time is it?"

Neither Fitz nor I wanted to move the discussion to some public place before we had accomplished our objective. Fitz quickly offered that he had a six-pack in his trunk and promptly left to get it, but warm beer wasn't exactly our idea of a thirst quencher. "I can handle that," Fred offered, reaching for the hand-held fire extinguisher mounted just outside the door. He pulled the pin, squeezed the handle and sprayed the six-pack cans with foam from the extinguisher. "Just a little thing I learned in Nam," he said. "Your chilled beer is now ready for our enjoyment."

That little exhibition seemed to complete the change in Fred's mood. He appeared to brighten, to return to his normal, confident self, and we began talking optimistically about the future. When we finally walked out just before dawn, Fred was his old dynamic self, convinced that he was the one destined to fulfill his dream for a successful Federal Express. He would not tender his resignation at the board meeting.

OUR NEXT STEP

Fitz and I suspected that some of the investors and lenders were pressing for Fred's resignation. We were going to do everything in our power to stop any effort to force his resignation, but we weren't sure what that would entail. An early-morning breakfast at the nearby Denny's restaurant would be a good place to begin hatching a plan. First, we would confront Charlie Lea. We had learned from Fred that he and Charlie had had a conversation earlier the previous evening. Fred did not divulge the exact nature of the discussion, but we felt this might have had some bearing on his decision to resign.

We drove the short distance to Charlie's hotel, called his room on the house phone, and received a sleepy response to our effort. "Mike Fitzgerald and I are in the lobby and would like to talk with you before today's board meeting," I explained. "May we come to your room?"

"What is this about?" Charlie inquired.

"It's about Fred."

"OK, come on up. It's room 324."

Charlie, still in his nighttime attire, greeted us at the door. Of all the backers of Federal Express, Charlie was absolutely my favorite. However, whether he was the messenger, as I assumed, or had played a part in Fred's threatened resignation, I was angry with my friend. Moreover, Fitz and I had been up all night and probably looked like two escapees from the local asylum, which undoubtedly gave Charlie reason to question our sanity.

"Fred is not going to resign at the board meeting," I immediately blurted out, "and he is not going to leave the company. You and the rest of the investors are not going to get rid of him without a fight. If Fred goes, the planes will not fly."

"Wait a minute—what is this all about? Who said anything about getting rid of Fred?" Charlie responded. "Fred did mention that he had an offer to run an airline in England, but that does not mean that anyone is trying to get rid of him."

Fitz was normally the excitable one, but this time he attempted to calm me down. "Hold on—let's tell Charlie where we have been all night," he suggested. Then he began patiently explaining the events of the past night. Fitz said, "Look, Charlie, we understand that Fred is going to either take a lesser position in the company or get canned. You and the others do not a have a clue about the repercussions that action is going to produce within Federal Express."

Charlie denied the allegation, saying, "Fred is exhausted and depressed, but he still has a role to play. He needs time to recuperate, to be out of the public's view and the eye of the storm. Because of the things that are happening, he just needs to take a simple leave of absence."

"Charlie, that is simply not true," Fitz responded. "Everybody knows that if Fred takes that sabbatical, he is gone—the polite way to get him out the door."

"Oh, no, no," Charlie assured us, "things will calm down and Fred will be welcomed back."

Fitz, now with his Irish ire aroused, remained on the offensive. "Look," he said, "I don't believe it and I don't think that you really believe it."

The conversation proceeded on a serious note, Fitz and I explaining our position and Charlie, now fully awake, appearing to weigh all sides of the situation. It was a difficult time for each of us. Finally, Fitz and I decided to end the confrontation, stop by our homes, freshen up a bit, and prepare for the challenging day ahead.

STEPPING UP TO THE PLATE

When I got to the office, I learned that the outside directors were already meeting in special session. Meanwhile, I held my own meeting with the other senior officers in the office adjacent to the conference room. Fitz and I brought everyone up-to-date. The others concurred with our appraisal and agreed to the second part of our plan.

In order to make certain that there was no misinterpretation of our position, we typed a letter putting the board of directors on notice that if Fred were forced to step down or resign, most of the senior management group would also resign. The letter was signed by the following senior vice presidents: Michael Basch, Arthur Bass, Vince Fagan, Michael Fitzgerald, Tuck Morse, James Riedmeyer, Tucker Taylor, and myself. We sent the letter into the conference room, requesting that the contents be included in the deliberations of the board's special session.

We spent the remainder of the morning waiting for some word from the board. Deep down each of us wondered what the afternoon would bring. It was quite likely we would all be unemployed before evening. Had we made the right decision? Absolutely! We felt great allegiance to our leader, and no one in the room was going to back down now. Even if our letter was not important to the outside board members, it was important to us.

If the adventure was over for us, so be it; without Fred's leadership, the cost-cutting mentality would surely sink the business anyway. I remembered a cartoon that someone had passed around during an earlier meeting. It showed a manager pointing to a chart of costs sloping consistently downward. The caption read, "We have reached the ultimate in cost reduction, we are out of business." None of us wanted to be around to see that happen to Federal Express or to be a party to that scenario.

In our crowded room, we talked some more and we waited, and we waited. What was taking so long? We were growing impatient. Eventually, Charlie came out of the conference room looking for Art. He did not look too pleased about the situation and did not want to answer any questions. He only wanted Art to come into their closed-door session.

When Art returned about 30 minutes later, he described the discussion that had taken place in the conference room. "Well, first, the directors in the room wanted to know if the remaining senior officers were truly committed to tendering their resignation as they had indicated in the letter," Art explained. "And I answered in the affirmative, outlining the reasons behind the decision. Then one of the outside directors said, 'Well, Fred is leaving and that has already been decided. General Estes will remain the chief executive and we are prepared to make you president of Federal Express. Can you convince the other senior officers to retract their resignations?'"

Art replied, "You are missing the point. Most of the people in this company are here because of Fred. Furthermore, the question of my ability to convince any other senior officer to change his mind about the resignation is irrelevant." Art then explained that he did not intend to stay with the company in any position if Fred no longer remained the guiding force of Federal Express. "They made some comment about this being a once-in-a-lifetime opportunity," Art added, "and said that I should think seriously about the offer. I replied that under the conditions they had proposed, I was not interested, thanked them for their confidence in me, got up, and left the meeting."

The outside directors were obviously struggling with the situation. Apparently, they had not counted on the rebellious nature of the tightly knit guerrilla camp. Their offer to make Art the president was a bargaining ploy that might have been successful under other circumstances; he was certainly a qualified, caring, and truly compassionate person, respected and admired by all of the senior officers. Art said he had a feeling that the directors thought he was an easygoing patsy who would cave in to their offer and help them out of the dilemma. Well, they had certainly misjudged Art!

Sometime later, Charlie again came out of the conference room, this time looking for Fitz. "They attempted to assure me that if Fred goes away or goes on a sabbatical, nothing serious will happen to the company," Fitz told us later. "I don't believe the outside directors care one iota about Fred or what happens to him, or for that matter, to us. In my opinion, their only concern is that if we leave now, they might lose their money—it is all about money and power." Hearing Fitz's description of the infuriating interview, we were more committed than ever to our course of action.

In the end, Charlie announced that Estes was resigning and Fred would assume his position as chairman of the board. Furthermore, provided the senior management group approved, Art would be named president and chief operating officer.

Charlie, recalling the circumstances of that day, said, "It was important that the senior executives made their stand. It gave the clear message that we didn't have a lot of choice in the matter. It was just a dreadful time. All the board members discussed the situation together, but I was of the opinion that Fred needed to play a role in the company, especially after the senior officers all lined up behind him."

"We needed to convince Fred to stay," Charlie explained, "to get Art to take on the role of president, and to retain the chief executive position in a special three-man committee. That was a pretty tall order given the emotions of everybody at that particular time."

The board appointed Charlie to head the new committee that, with Larry Lawrence and Phil Greer, would represent the board for important policy matters until a new chief executive officer could be hired. While Charlie worked directly with Fred on critical issues requiring executive attention, Larry and Phil continued the search for a new CEO. Charlie avoided most of the unnecessary discussions by meeting with the other two members only the evening before our regularly scheduled board meetings. "As improbable as it sounds," Charlie says, "the company ran pretty well, given that totally oddball arrangement."

We supported Fred because he valued the people building the company. Fred was our chosen leader to guide the company. There are times when you just have to step up to the plate, and if need be, even to put your entire career on the line for what you believe is right; that is exactly what we had just done. It was a good feeling!

Three Division Offices

y term as general manager of operations ended as the management group agreed to the structure proposed by the board's executive committee. I was nearing the completion of my three-year employment contract anyway and was relieved that Art would be the one to take over my position. I was confident he would do a good job. Perhaps this was a propitious time for me to move on, but on the other hand, Federal Express was still an exciting company with an improving financial condition. It would be interesting to see what we could do when the company became profitable. It was time to have a serious talk with Fred.

I was astonished when Fred did not even mention the strange events of the preceding days. Estes suddenly no longer existed; gone were his Mercedes, his private parking spot, his papers, and his persona, all without a single comment from Fred. In fact, our meeting progressed as if the resignation threat and the board's attempt at ousting our founder had never occurred. As far as I know, he never even acknowledged the stand that the management group had taken. I was seeing another side of our leader—an emerging attitude of executive infallibility and a certain aloofness in his personality that left no room for personal gratitude.

My meeting with Fred progressed as though nothing of importance had occurred to alter the plan outlined in the draft memo the day before the board meeting. The number-one priority, according to Fred, was to provide additional training for the field personnel, improve the regional field operating units, enhance working conditions at the stations, and upgrade the temporary airport facilities hastily acquired over the past two years. Fitz, Tucker, and I, in conjunction with Vince, were going to plan the next iteration of the management shuffle.

With Fred's approval, we established three operating divisions to manage all of the areas outside the Memphis corporate office. In Fred's words, the new structure positioned the operating executives closer to the field personnel and customer service functions, partly to appease the lending banks and partly to improve administrative control of company operations. By the end of May, Fitz and I were preparing to pack up our households and transplant our families to new homes, Fitz to the East Coast and I to the West Coast. Along with Tucker, who remained in Memphis, the three of us were the new divisional senior vice presidents, charged with Fred's mandate to improve field facilities and operating conditions.

I left Memphis with mixed emotions. On one hand, I was pleased to be going to the San Francisco Bay area and delighted with the opportunity offered by the new challenge. On the other hand, the first stage of this exciting venture was ending, and leaving Memphis would isolate me from the high-level discussions of the previous three years. I would continue serving on the board of directors, but even there, the issues were now certain to be more mundane. I was not too certain that I had made the best decision. Furthermore, I was once again subjecting my family to another unwelcome move.

THE WESTERN DIVISION

Fred was right about the condition of the field operating facilities. Major airlines and established airfreight forwarders occupy the prime cargo locations at most airports. The airport ramp space initially granted to Federal Express was far from optimal, reflecting the airport managers' commitment to the established tenants, the uncertain future of our new entity, and our own inability to afford new construction. The fact that we frequently were late paying our landing fees did nothing to bolster our reputation with the airports. Our off-airport facilities, the city stations, primarily noted for their low rent, offered little in the way of marketing visibility or ultimate operating effectiveness. We could fix those problems.

The bright spot turned out to be the quality and motivation of the couriers, customer service agents, supervisors, and managers of the field stations, most of whom were young, passionate, and highly skilled representatives for the company. In fact, the average age of the entire workforce at Federal Express was about 27 and most of them were highly educated. We even had couriers with doctorate degrees who seemed quite content with their jobs. People were careful about expenses. Productivity levels were acceptable, considering that some of the vans were traveling up to 125 miles per day because of the low density. The salespeople were well trained and highly motivated, working diligently to increase the package volume. As time went on, they became the nucleus of the expanding field operations and key to maintaining a binding relationship with our customer base. Moreover, the relaxed atmosphere in the divisions was definitely a pleasant change from the Memphis madhouse.

Shortly after we opened the Western Division office, an unexpected shipment arrived. It was a table for our conference room. Attached to the table, sent by one of the executives at REA Express, was a note saying, "As we are regretfully forced to terminate operations, kindly accept this table from our board room as a token of our friendship and respect, with our sincere hopes that you and your organization make better use of it than we have." The Railway Express Agency, originally owned by eighty-six railroads, had survived for 46 years and in some ways was the Federal Express of its day. It made me realize that even a corporation that was once a major force in the express business—an organization with the backing of the largest transportation companies in America—could ultimately fail. It was a sobering thought.

IN DEFAULT

Although the outlook for Federal was improving, we were in default on the scheduled payments to CCEC at the end of May 1975. Commercial Credit threatened to repossess the planes if the loan payments were not brought up-to-date. Charlie, Pete, and Art traveled to CCEC's headquarters in Baltimore to discuss the issues. "After lunch," according to Pete, "we entered the huge office of John Sheehan, the head of CCEC, and were seated right in front of his desk. About a football field back are all the other CCEC executives, leaning against the far wall, getting as far away from us as they possibly could."

Sheehan had a Federal Express file on his desk with two sheets of paper in it, one of them a financial statement from six months earlier. Sheehan then sent for and briefly reviewed the new business plan for fiscal 1976. He responded with disbelief, complaining that the company was still making the same unbelievable projections that it had made in the past. Charlie assured him that Federal Express was now doing much better and was on track to make the new projections.

At that point, Sheehan asked, "Well how much are these planes worth?" Art gave a figure well below the value of the CCEC loan and backed it up with elegant reasoning, explaining that if CCEC were to repossess the Falcons, it would be very expensive to convert the planes back to their original passenger configuration. Art added that the market for used Falcons was depressed, and it would be difficult to sell the planes.

Sheehan, exasperated by the situation, looked at the three senior officers of Federal Express and said, "All right, I think I'll just give you enough rope to hang yourself." "That was the end of the meeting," according to Charlie, "and we had a reprieve. Federal Express was built on crazy things like that."

26

Just Step out of the Way

I n June the board of directors took preliminary steps toward an initial public offering, then ran into a few roadblocks. Warrants held by the lending banks and awarded during the three rounds of private placements now gave them a claim on nearly 25 percent of the shares. Fred questioned the legitimacy of the banks' claim to the warrants and charged that the banks had reneged on their obligation to return the warrants. Charges and counter-charges resulted in open confrontations, with neither side yielding. Meanwhile, in light of the exasperating situation, the public offering was deferred indefinitely.

THE YEAR OF TRANSITION

The year 1975, the third year after beginning the small-package service, marked a watershed for the company. It was the year of transition from a startup venture to a completely functional operating company with a full complement of modified Falcon aircraft, an established nationwide network with facilities in nearly every major U.S. market area, and a growing reputation for reliable overnight service. July, the second month of the fiscal year, was our first profitable month. Federal Express was now a company capable of generating enough cash to fund continued expansion of its operations and paying for ongoing improvements to its service. The dream was actually becoming a reality.

Our next major corporate challenge was in the legislative arena. During 1975 the increasing volume of small packages began to strain the carrying capacity of the Falcon fleet. We were flying two aircraft into our larger markets to handle the nightly volume. We could mitigate that problem only by introducing aircraft with greater weight and volume capacity. Without larger aircraft, future growth would be curtailed, not by the market demand, not by our capability in a free economy, but by regulatory limitations. We needed to find ways to expand our fleet, to seek further regulatory relief, or to just stop growing—but the last was not an enticing alternative.

In September, Federal Express filed an application with the CAB requesting an exemption from the capacity limitations in order to operate five DC-9-15 cargo planes to our major markets. In all-cargo configuration, the DC-9 had a payload capacity more than twice that of the Falcon. The DC-9 far exceeded the limit to qualify for exemption from CAB economic regulation, but we hoped that the agency might grant emergency relief to allow our continued expansion.

We asserted that our service was valuable to the public, citing our transport of essential commercial documents and products, critical shipments of human transplant organs, and other extremely time-sensitive items. The entire aviation industry objected to our petition, and in December the CAB denied our request, noting that it was powerless to grant our exemption because of the limits Congress had placed on its authority.

December 1975 was also the month that settled the matter of the forged loan guarantee documents for the Union Bank. At his trial, Fred testified that as president of the Enterprise board and with supporting letters from his sisters, he had authority to commit the board. After 10 hours of deliberation, he was acquitted. If convicted, he would have faced a prison term of up to five years.

WORKING FOR CARGO DEREGULATION

Freed from the overhanging threat, Fred now became more determined than ever to seek a change to the outmoded regulations. This time there was more hope, as the government representatives in Washington began to sense a need for an overhaul of the restrictive airline regulations.

Fred once more returned to Washington and, along with Nat, presented our case before the Senate and House Subcommittees on Aviation in April 1976, arguing that the outmoded regulations, intended primarily for passenger service, were stifling the cargo carriers, and pointing out that Federal Express was not asking for anything from the government except to "step out of the way." In response, the Senate subcommittee drafted a bill to liberalize the cargo regulations that was immediately attacked as special interest legislation for the benefit of Federal Express. "The effort was opposed by the Teamsters Union and by ALPA," Nat recalls. "Both saw it as a real threat to a system in which they had a strong vested interest. Flying Tiger Line, already a certificated and large all-cargo carrier, vehemently opposed the pleadings."

Tuck, who accompanied the Washington delegation, carried around the Aviation Act of 1938, a 350-page book containing all the CAB regulations. Fred argued with the chief counsel, who was giving us a hard time. Frustrated, Fred grabbed the book, ripped it in half and threw it on the chief counsel's desk, saying, "That is what I think of your arguments. You don't understand the law, and you are jeopardizing our company by being difficult."

By chartering supplemental aircraft, opening a "bleed-off" hub in Pittsburgh, double-turning some flights, and trucking packages from some of the nearby locations, we were just barely able to keep pace with the growing volumes. However, it was clear that this was only a temporary solution. Despite the capacity challenges, our fiscal year ending in May 1976 saw gross revenue more than 70 percent above the previous year. Moreover, the company produced a net profit of $3.6 million for the year, and continued to be profitable from that point forward.

We then mounted an intensive media campaign, sending material to over 40,000 of our customers, asking their support for the permissive legislation. We sent promotion packets to members of Congress, urging support of the bill. We provided form letters to our employees so that they and their relatives and friends could write their congressional representatives in support of the bill. The senior management group appeared on television talk shows, contacted groups of business leaders, met with a variety of state and federal legislative staffs, and spoke at various business functions.

In July, I had a memorable experience at a business luncheon in Seattle. During my presentation I noted that Federal Express had just completed its first year of profitability. One questioner, who obviously had spent a little too much time at the refreshment stand, stood up and said, "I have worked in the cargo department of United Airlines for over 20 years, and I speak from experience when I say that you are a damn liar. There is no way that you or anyone else can make a profit operating those small planes to transport cargo." Our host quickly apologized for the ill-conceived attack, but the remark helped drive home my point—we needed to change the outdated regulations.

In the end, the "special interest legislation," which was passed without dissent in the Senate, was not even voted upon in the House. The "Federal Express Bill" died, and we were still no further along in our attempt to provide rational and economical lift to match the growing demand for our expedited small-package service.

Over the next few months, we continued to fly wingtip-to-wingtip to the heavier markets at the outer limits of our service area and to supplement those flights with propeller-driven chartered aircraft to the closer-in cities. At the peak of this frustrating period, we were chartering up to fifty other aircraft, including what must have been every operational DC-3 then in existence in the country.

It was actually a beautifully nostalgic sight to see all the "gooney birds" parked on the ramp in Memphis. One evening, while on one of my nocturnal visits to the hub, a pilot of one of the DC-3s approached me with a grin, saying, "Mr. Frock, I have just added a new feature to our bird that I would like you to see." He led me over to his aircraft, where we entered the rear cargo door and climbed the steep incline to the cockpit. Pointing to a capped tube protruding from the starboard side of the plane, he said, "This little addition is saving me nearly an hour on the route we are running for you."

I just had to ask the obvious question, "How can that little tube save you that much time? What's the trick?"

The pilot smiled. "Well, you know this plane has been around for quite a long time, and we were burning so much oil that we were having to make a stop on the inbound leg just to add oil, but now the copilot is able to add oil to the engines in flight through this tube." Even our chartered friends were going that extra mile to make certain that the packages made it to the hub on time.

ABSOLUTELY, POSITIVELY OVERNIGHT

The driving forces behind the company's rapid expansion in the latter part of the 1970s was due in large part to Vince Fagan's dynamic marketing and sales programs. With the growth in package volumes, the ability to respond to all afternoon pick-up requests became more and more difficult, and customers frequently expressed anxiety while they awaited a scheduled pickup. To address these concerns, Vince decided to experiment with customer drop boxes and attendant-operated drive-up kiosks located at shopping malls. These new drop-off points helped to alleviate some of the concerns, and the drop boxes soon became hugely popular, eventually numbering in the thousands of locations.

However, some shippers were not completely comfortable putting their important packages in the unmanned drop boxes. Vince's response to the customer concerns was the Customer Convenience Center. These storefront facilities, typically located on the ground floor, make Federal Express's service accessible to walk-in customers. Operationally, the centers provide a means for couriers to combine a multitude of shipments on a single end-of-day pickup—convenient for the customers and effective for the company.

Federal Express's first three ads were, in Vince's words, "informational commercials that described our system, and they explained how Federal Express differed from freight forwarders, REA and UPS." By the end of 1976, however, Vince felt it was time to re-evaluate the introductory presentations.

Vince and our advertising agency conducted numerous focus group sessions to gain a better understanding of the priority shippers' needs and concerns and to chart a new course for the promotions. The sessions clearly showed that shippers were tiring of the unreliable service offered by most carriers. The priority shippers were most concerned with reliability: They wanted assurance that their very important special documents and packages would "absolutely, positively" arrive on time. Our customers were once again telling us about our business, and we were listening.

The marketing research generated the theme for the ads and other promotions that keynoted the promotional programs into the early 1980s. These wonderfully humorous ads featured the internal heroes of the companies that were Federal Express's customers: those employees responsible for moving priority shipments quickly and reliably—the secretaries, mailroom employees, shipping clerks, and worried managers. *"Federal Express—When it absolutely, positively has to be there overnight."* It was a carefully researched and beautifully created response to the concerns of the marketplace, a masterpiece of marketing expertise and proficiency. The ads, along with several of the other pieces created by Ally and Gargano, won numerous Clio Awards, the world's most recognized international advertising awards competition. *Advertising Age* also honored the series as one of the fifty best commercials of the decade.

When we first attempted to air the ads, the major networks were skeptical and required proof of our service levels. We eventually copied and sent hundreds of airbills with the shipper and delivery address blanked out before they would agree to run the commercials. Even then, the networks urged softening the message, but Vince refused. Considering some of the promotions that currently bombard our screens, one can only wonder if these networks are now as rigorous in researching proof of claims.

In our fourth year of operations, we saw another surge in profits. Revenues increased by 45 percent over the previous year, and net profit for the fiscal year increased to nearly $7.9 million. In June 1977, while Fitz and I continued working in our respective division offices, Mike replaced Tucker as head of the Southern Division, freeing Tucker for another project. Wes Terry, then senior vice president of industrial relations, assumed responsibility for the newly created Central Division.

THE FINAL REGULATORY HURDLE

Fred was unwavering in his belief that we would get the regulatory relief we needed to continue the growth of the small-package service. Anticipating the right to operate larger aircraft, he assigned the senior managers supplemental projects. We were on the verge of exceeding even the most optimistic plan for Fred's crazy concept.

The CAB apparently agreed with Fred, even though the certificated airlines and labor unions did not. As early as 1975, the CAB had issued a report saying it could no longer justify entry controls or public utility–type price controls. In-state flights by Southwest Airlines in Texas as well as Air California and Pacific Southwest Airlines in California, over which the CAB lacked jurisdiction, provided examples of the broader array of services the airline industry could offer its customers if market regulations were eased or removed and carriers were allowed to compete. Fares charged by these airlines were about 50 percent below those on identical routes flown by regulated airlines across state lines. These operations also demonstrated that significantly lower fares would generate a new wave of demand.

In August 1977 Congressman Glenn Anderson introduced House bill 8813, intended to provide greater freedom of entry and greater pricing flexibility for all airlines, as well as automatic certification for the existing cargo airlines. Alfred Kahn, who became CAB chairman that year, appeared in support of open entry for all-cargo carriers and argued that the board should give all airlines greater pricing freedom and easier access to routes. On October 20 Senator Howard Cannon arranged to have an amendment containing provisions for air cargo deregulation attached to an unrelated bill (HR 6010) sent to the Senate.

The Senate and House both approved the bill by voice vote without opposition, and President Jimmy Carter signed it into law on November 9, 1977, changing the Federal Aviation Act of 1958 to include a section titled "Certification for All-Cargo Air Service." Federal Express and many other all-cargo airlines that had been operating at least one year prior to the enactment of the law were grandfathered in and now were free to choose their own routes, set their own rates, and fly the planes that best suited their operating requirements.

It had been a long, intense struggle with an outcome that seemed nearly unimaginable or at least highly unlikely at the outset. It was, however a virtual case study in how the entrepreneurial spirit and the American free enterprise system can ultimately combine to create an outcome that benefits everyone.

Federal Express immediately invited the treasurer of United Airlines to Memphis, where Tuck negotiated a final agreement to purchase thirteen of their used Boeing 727 cargo planes. Tuck then offered an escorted tour of the hub, where the disinterested treasurer confided that United had lost its shirt on cargo. A bit smug about dumping their losing fleet, he questioned how Federal could expect to make money transporting small packages. Tuck asked, "What are your rates for cargo?" The treasurer responded that they averaged 20 cents a pound. "Our rates average $3.60 per pound," Tuck explained, "and that is why we are so pleased to have your discards."

United converted the planes at its San Francisco service facility, where I had the rewarding pleasure of witnessing the modifications and seeing the rollout of the newly configured purple and orange additions to our fleet. The first plane arrived in Memphis on January 14, 1978, 66 days after deregulation.

OUR INITIAL PUBLIC OFFERING

Deregulation of the air cargo industry changed the outlook for the company and allowed the banks to view Federal Express in a more positive light. The future of the company now seemed assured. All parties began a genuinely cooperative effort to recapitalize the company, to make amends for past greed and inequities, and to proceed with the initial public offering. After voting to return the mantle of chief executive officer to Fred, Charlie and I resigned from the board of directors to make room for additional outside directors.

Fred arranged for Federal Express employees to purchase up to 220,000 shares of the public offering at a slightly discounted price. Over half of our loyal employees placed orders for stock shares, indicating their continued confidence in the company. On April 12, 1978, the public offering was completed. The successful offering sold 783,000 shares of Federal Express stock at a price of $24 per share, raising $18.8 million. The employees placed orders for 635,000 shares, which had to be proportionately reduced to fit the agreed-on reserve. The shares sold at the public offering have appreciated today, after all the stock splits, by over 10,000 percent.

Fred, following completion of the offering, gathered the senior management group together to thank everyone for his past contributions and to urge our continued efforts toward the success of the company. Since our management shares could not be sold for a stipulated amount of time, Fred quipped, "Congratulations, you are no longer insolvent, you are merely illiquid."

The company had beaten all the odds, overcome seemingly insurmountable obstacles, encountered enough near-disasters to last a lifetime, and achieved the impossible. For all of those involved in the epic struggle, it was finally the season of Light.

PART V

Transformation and Separation
May 1978 to January 1982

27

From Caterpillar
to Butterfly

F ederal Express illustrates the importance of transformation," argues Charles Brandon. "Originally, we
were really operating a prototype system, though few
of us realized that in the beginning. Our analytical and
communication applications were generally copied or
acquired from others, utilizing off-the-shelf, almost prim-
itive systems." FedEx became a leader in applying new
technology to the business of transportation, only after
going through an extensive transformation.

CENTRALIZED CUSTOMER
SERVICE SYSTEM

Initially, our ground operations were modeled on United
Parcel Service. However, we learned there was a profound
and important difference between UPS and Federal
Express. UPS had a large customer base, so its pickup routes were very dense, highly regular, and generally
composed of fixed, prescheduled stops. Irregular or
infrequent shippers could contact the company and, by
paying the service charge for a full week, schedule a
pickup for the *next business day*.

Federal Express initially had far fewer customers, and
our courier van routes changed daily in response to customer needs. Rapid reaction to customer calls, real-time
dispatching, and sophisticated communications systems
were of utmost importance.

Our customer service agents, located at each city station, received all incoming calls for pickups, as well as customer service calls and administrative calls. They also tended the counters where customers picked up or dropped off packages, and occasionally became involved in tracing packages. Our agents became overloaded as volumes increased, and it was getting harder to provide courteous service to our customers. Tucker Taylor received a new assignment in mid-1976 to find a long-term solution to the station problems.

Most field managers thought we would benefit from a centralized telephone system to handle customer calls. Others, concerned about losing our personal touch, favored keeping most of the activity at the stations. To resolve the customer acceptance question, we decided to test a new customer call system—one based on the scheduled airline customer reservations systems. Tucker selected Newark, New Jersey, one of the largest stations, for the test.

The field managers became instant converts. This change allowed our personnel to focus attention on improving their response to customers. We then added the system in eleven more cities, expanded our computer support, and provided speedier access to key information.

Then Federal developed its first centralized Customer Service Center in Memphis. Kathy Crockett, supported by Charles's group, managed the project. Kathy, steeped in the dynamic culture of Federal Express, was one of those people you call upon when it absolutely, positively has to be done right. The Memphis Customer Service Center opened in late 1977 and in less than a year was handling all customer calls for the entire nationwide Federal Express network.

REACHING FOR A PACKAGE TRACKING SYSTEM

Fred continually pushed the management group to develop new approaches that would improve service and outdistance our competition. This outlook gave birth to a rich inventory of innovative solutions, some more successful than others. Mike Basch, then head of the Corporate Development group, initiated a series of invitational meetings to ask customers how we could serve them better. They were especially interested in the following items:

- Getting the packages there on time
- If a service failure occurs, knowing when the package will be delivered
- Expanding the geographic coverage
- Furnishing an airbill that is easy to use
- Providing accurate and timely billing
- Offering the service at a reasonable price

Armed with this information, we started looking at alternatives to the hand-generated airbills. Priority small-package shippers wanted faster, more reliable service than UPS customers, who were accustomed to shipment times of two to five days. Those shippers expected us to meet our service commitments. If a failure did occur, they wanted assurance we could identify the problem and initiate corrective actions—that meant developing a real-time tracking system from the point of origin to delivery.

Mike's group created the *STAR* (System-wide Tracking and Recording) system to trace packages, using machines very similar to ones service stations employed for recording fuel purchases. It made airbill preparation a lot simpler for our customers and improved its readability, but we just could not get accurate scans of the information on the airbill needed for billing the shipment, so we abandoned that idea. What next?

Bar codes seemed a good idea, but we had to wait for the technology to catch up with our conceptual design. The first bar-code systems were demonstrated as early as June 1974, but practical applications for our requirements became available only later.

PROJECT BUTTERFLY

In 1977 Charles was selected to head our Information Systems Division and assigned the task of developing a unique system to handle our increasing volume of high-speed transactions. Charles's group led the task of reinventing the company from the ground up in *Project Butterfly*, using the terms "caterpillar," "chrysalis," and "butterfly" to denote the stages of the transformation.

Charles's new system would allow the Customer Service Center to transmit pickup information directly to the courier van. The courier could enter destination data at the time of pickup so the central hub could automatically sort each package. We would be able to track packages through the network and have a timely, accurate way to bill for the shipment. It was an exciting concept that promised to provide enhanced reliability and meaningful customer service.

There was just one problem—such a system had never before been designed for our type of business. IBM had created one for the passenger airlines, to aid customers who were calling to check fares, make or change reservations, and find out if flights were on time or late. Howard Bedford had developed the software that became standard for these systems in the airline industry. Charles's approach to meeting the challenge at Federal Express was to hire Bedford and the senior members of his team to develop the new system.

Bedford was delighted with the idea, but would not live in Memphis. He proposed Colorado Springs, the home of the North American Air Defense Command and not far from United Airlines' giant Apollo System headquarters with literally thousands of skilled programmers. In a few months, Federal Express opened the doors of the Colorado Springs research and development center with a staff of more than one hundred technicians.

Within three months, Bedford presented us with a computer demonstration of COSMOS, the Customer Oriented Service and Management Operating System, for our review. It was so appealing, we wanted the system installed immediately. "Just a minute," Bedford cautioned, "this is only a demo. We still have to do the programming, design the peripherals, develop a prototype network, test the prototype with sample data, scale up the system to cover your projected needs, and incorporate the capability to expand the system. In about two years, we should be ready for deployment."

Disappointed with the complexities of obtaining our dream system, but confident in Bedford's ability to produce the finished product, we had no problem authorizing the continued effort.

To complete system design, we had to develop a digital communications link between the Customer Service Center and the courier vans. We envisioned a computer video display in each of the vans, linked to a computer in the centralized dispatch facility on the same channel used for voice communications. Eventually, Federal found a product whose maker could modify it to fit our needs.

Bedford's team continued its work in Colorado Springs, and by the second quarter of 1979 the new system was operational. COSMOS handled the customer pickup requests at the centralized Customer Service Center and provided information on a timely basis to and from the courier fleet via the digital communications link called DADS (for Digitally Assisted Dispatch System). As technology advanced, an electronic scanner was added so the courier could transfer the airbill information to the truck computer and transmit it to the central Customer Service Center as well as to the hub.

When the Internet and personal computer came along, Federal upgraded the system, allowing shippers to enter billing and delivery information directly on terminals located at their premises. There were a few false steps in the leadup to the final product, but these were not failures; they provided information that ultimately allowed us to progress to the next stage of development.

The message from our experience is this: We began by listening to our customers. That led us to investigate STAR machines and bar codes, which in turn led to preprinted airbills and ultimately to a much more sophisticated process. That is the pattern of evolution and transformation in business—the progressive stages of awareness, understanding, and integration that make up the cycle of development.

Mach 1 to Idle

ederal Express was maturing, transforming from an entrepreneurial, fast-paced, decentralized decision-making entity to a more tightly controlled and highly structured corporation. The company was beginning to lose some of its flexibility, to downplay the interchanging roles of the senior management group, and moving toward compartmentalization. Inevitably, territorial silos were rising, to the detriment of the some of the cooperation that characterized earlier years.

Fred, freed from most of his financial concerns and personal problems, was changing from primarily a charismatic leader to a tougher, no-nonsense corporate executive. He was beginning to have second thoughts about the decentralized division structure and was concerned that the division heads were creating too much autonomy and were building independent fiefdoms.

The purpose of decentralization was to empower our hands-on managers to make decisions based on their knowledge of the region and its special needs. For the most part, things functioned well for the first two years. Our productivity measurements, the service level reports, and the way we treated employees and customers were coordinated through regular monthly meetings. Geographic differences affected our operations, of course, but we never strayed from the company's founding principles.

During the third year, there were rumblings from the corporate office about differences between the divisions. "There were clearly differences in management styles," Mike Fitzgerald admits, "but that happens anywhere. People who run machines have different personalities, but that does not mean they run the machines differently." However, the new corporate managers who replaced the division heads were critical of the independent field operations, and the division managers in turn were concerned about the unrelenting growth of the corporate staff.

END OF THE DIVISION STRUCTURE

In February 1978 Fred chaired a contentious meeting held at one of the local Memphis restaurants. He ordered the division heads back to Memphis and announced the end of their reign. His criticism and assault, coming without any warning, surprised us. He announced a new field management organization that would operate under tight controls from the corporate office. Federal would become a totally centralized organization, with field managers operating only in response to corporate directives.

While Fred rarely issued a direct order, he was now proclaiming that this was the end of an era. Henceforth, he declared, everyone would "step out in military lockstep order" in response to his directives.

Fred was confirming that he was now finished with the legislative battles, was confident of the financial success of Federal Express, and was ready to assume complete operating control of the company. The division heads would be assigned new responsibilities within a few days.

Fred intended to centralize the organization and return all operating authority to Memphis. He did not want his former senior executives in control of the field operating divisions. Fitz observed, "Up to this time, we had been able to challenge Fred when he was wrong, and that did not fit well with his conception of a large public company. It did not make Fred feel warm and fuzzy to sit around a table with a bunch of guys that he had drunk beer with, and who knew where some of the weaknesses were." We knew more about Fred than we needed to know, and a great deal more than he wanted us to know.

At the time, the division heads felt that Smith should have discussed the issues with them beforehand, which had been the standard procedure. Peter Schutz maintains that to manage well in this era of accelerating change and competition, businesses must learn to decide like a democracy, so that they may subsequently implement like a dictatorship.

Fred handled the dictatorship part admirably, but ignored the democracy part. He sensed that if he sat down with us and explained the reasons for ending the divisional structure, we would question his judgment. "He was in his hook-'em-up mode," recalls Fitz, "and he wanted to get the job done, irrespective of our feelings. Fred actually made a very accurate assessment of our personalities and knew what our reactions would be. The real problem was that we were going from near Mach 1 to almost an idle—and that was what Fred intended."

Before the end of the fiscal year, I was back in Memphis, this time alone. My wife opted to remain in California. She had had enough of Federal Express, enough of the constant moving, enough of my perpetual absences, and enough of the constant shifts. We decided on a legal separation. The entire move away from corporate headquarters turned out to be a horrible mistake. I was deeply depressed and disillusioned, yet I had created the situation. Now, my relationship with Fred had suddenly deteriorated and I considered leaving the company. Fitz helped me to understand that there was still work to be done, and like the other senior executives, I did not want to leave a job unfinished.

Mike returned to managing the Memphis hub, Fitz was assigned to manage our ground vehicle fleet, and I continued to oversee the tactical planning for the large aircraft. Preparation for the fleet of large planes entailed a complete change in the package-handling processes. The Falcons were loaded and unloaded manually. Because the much larger B-727s are equipped with roller floors to handle full containers, mechanized handling systems are used. We needed to make major modifications to our Memphis hub and at every city station. Fortunately, the major airlines were eliminating most of their all-cargo operations, so we were able to acquire their loading and unloading equipment.

THE MEMPHIS SUPERHUB

As heads of the Southern Division, Tucker and later Mike had added to the capacity of the hub each time we expanded our service. However, our ability to handle the larger aircraft was a cause for concern, and Mike began a three-year project to build the Memphis "Superhub." "Fred originally believed we needed additional hubs at Colorado Springs, Chicago, and Newburgh, New York," Mike recalls, "so we spent nearly a year developing an operating plan for that concept. The conveyor and sort technology was readily available to process the packages through those hubs."

Mike Staunton, our flight controller; Charles; and others felt uneasy about the four-hub concept, so they decided to run a simulation. The Operations Research Department and the Scheduling Department concluded after all the iterations that the four-hub network wasn't feasible. Fred was the ultimate realist. He just said, "Let's make a 180-degree turn and get out of here." Federal would later open other hubs, but only after the package volumes in those regions reached substantially higher levels.

"When we dropped the four-hub concept, we had to invent a system to handle seven times the volume of any then existing hub, anywhere in the world," says Mike. "I didn't even remotely know how to do that. We tackled each problem separately and then went on to the next. Our main concern was how to avoid a delay while checking the aircraft weight and balance. These calculations, which determine the container loading sequence for each aircraft, cannot be completed until all of the containers for the plane are weighed. The cost of conventional scales at each container loading station was prohibitively expensive. Then one of the team said, 'I understand that weight is directly proportional to the expansion of the circumference of a bar of metal, and if we can somehow measure that expansion, we would know the weight.' Eventually, for a few hundred dollars at each station, we solved that problem."

However, after two years working on the Superhub, we still did not have on-time departures. Mike put in a "countdown clock" that related work assignments to the sorting cutoff time, but that wasn't enough to solve the problem. He ultimately realized that the employee's goals were diametrically opposed to the company's goals. The part-time sorters were working with a guarantee of two hours, and most of them were going home shortly after two hours, so there was no incentive to get the sort completed on time. Mike increased the guarantee to four hours, and within a month, the on-time departures went from under 50 percent to over 95 percent. Our employees were still helping us to understand how to do a better job of managing our assets.

PROPERTIES AND FACILITIES DEPARTMENT

Shortly after completing the plan for large-aircraft operations, I was reassigned to the Properties and Facilities Department. At last, I was away from the constant stress of the startup—the financial anxieties, the never ending demands to meet daily schedules, and the intense strain to keep up with the rapid growth. Now I could work at something resembling a normal pace. With my staff of fifty, we constructed a five-year facilities plan for each of the outlying cities, developed a standard station design, built handling facilities at numerous airports, added thirty to forty new locations annually, and designed a campus-style office park for our corporate support staff. However, Fitz was right: Compared to the preceding years, it felt like I was running at idle. There was no spark, no excitement, and no challenge. It was not a good position for an entrepreneurial spirit.

OPERATION TORSO

As fate would have it, other business opportunities caught the attention of our imaginative leader. One Saturday morning, Smith assembled the entire senior management group at the Peabody Hotel in downtown Memphis. Perhaps he too was feeling the lack of excitement. Fred was always one to look to the future and make new use of the company's expertise and assets. He noted that our growing fleet of large aircraft, which now included the 727s and seven new Boeing 737s (and would soon include wide-body DC-10s), sat idle during many of the daylight hours and most weekends. He proposed Project Torso to evaluate a passenger charter service that would make use of these planes when they were not committed to the package service.

By the end of the meeting, senior management received new marching orders to develop the operating details for Torso. I always marveled at the way the group responded to Fred's ideas.

The senior managers often seamlessly shifted their focus, coordinated their activities, and headed in a new direction almost instantaneously. Federal Express applied for permissive scheduled passenger authority, initially between Chicago's Midway airport and up to twenty-four other cities. But that was just the beginning.

Days after the Peabody meeting, Fred and I traveled to New Jersey. Conrail was selling a long narrow stretch of land on the west shore of the Hudson River directly opposite Manhattan. Smith's extended plan for the passenger service involved the purchase of this parcel for a private airport. He had also considered a hydrofoil to shuttle passengers between New York City and the new airport. Several officials in New Jersey pledged their complete support. When the FAA refused our request to operate the proposed airfield, Smith suggested that passenger charters from Newark airport, combined with a hydrofoil shuttle from Manhattan, would be interesting.

Fitz, Art, and I traveled to Frankfurt and watched Lufthansa convert its passenger planes to cargo carriers each night, then back to passenger configuration each morning. The QC (quick-change) system worked, but the seats always had to return to the same plane, as there were slight differences in the dimensions of each aircraft. That meant that we could not substitute another plane if a mechanical problem occurred. In the end, we decided to abandon Project Torso, but Smith never stopped searching for ways to expand Federal Express and challenge our resourcefulness.

INTERNATIONAL OPERATIONS

Perhaps sensing the frustrations that some of the original management executives now felt in the "idle" mode, or just wanting to redirect our entrepreneurial instincts, Fred once again initiated an organizational change early in 1980. I was on vacation at the time; when I returned to my office in the Properties Department, it was occupied by my replacement.

Once again, Fred made the change without providing for information sharing between the retiree and the replacement. When Art Bass took over my general manager position, we did not have an opportunity to work out a transition plan. When we received the mandate to close our division offices, there was no provision for meeting with our replacements to discuss the ongoing projects. This was really beginning to disturb me. A sudden transition disrupts ongoing projects and is confusing for the departmental staff. Experience teaches that whenever department managers are changed, there should be a period to coordinate the transition.

Art and I initiated our own dialogue near the end of February and in one of his important "red memos," Fred announced that I would begin developing a "comprehensive operating plan for a Western Europe/US express service." This new assignment came as a complete surprise to me, and while I was pleased with what I considered an important new assignment, I did not have the foggiest notion of when or how Fred intended to begin this venture.

Federal first attempted international service in 1978, after receiving authority from the Canadian Transport Commission. Canadian Pacific Express, Ltd., via connections in Buffalo and Syracuse, initially handled our cross-border transportation, customs brokerage, and Canadian ground operations, providing service to Toronto and Montreal. In July 1979 we transferred the air and Canadian ground portion of our cross-border operations to Air Canada, with Cansica, Inc., a Canadian customs broker, performing the package clearance services.

Although I knew a little about the Canadian service, I had never looked at the details of the operation. In fact, I knew very little about the field of international commerce. I was not even sure who was in charge of the Canadian operation, but I figured that Air Canada and Cansica could help me understand some of the complexities of transporting packages between countries. So I flew off to Canada to begin my education on the nuances of international trade.

29

Concordes, Dirigibles, and Separation

During the remainder of 1980 and into the following year, I spent much of my time in Canada and Western Europe, returning to my base in Memphis to write and issue reports, arrange for upcoming trips, and gradually develop a concept for service to Western Europe. This was like reliving the stimulating experiences of the startup. It was perhaps even more interesting and rewarding because Federal Express was already well known and highly respected in the European business community.

The company now transported packages of up to 70 pounds and shipments of up to 150 pounds, which mandated a different design for our courier vans. Fitz's design now included high-cube courier vans with diesel engines produced in Western Europe, and he and I made frequent transatlantic trips together. We visited business executives, transport companies, and truck and engine manufacturers and were welcomed with open arms. We had little contact with the day-to-day function of the company, but that did not bother us in the least. We were back in the entrepreneurial mode, out of the exasperating idleness, and certain that our efforts would be the base for great things in the future.

However, I soon realized that the European market was very different from the one we had nurtured in the United States. For example, United Parcel had begun surface operations in Germany in 1976, delivering packages overnight to half of the country and providing second-day service for the rest. When UPS applied its U.S. operating methods and personnel practices to the German workforce, cultural clashes abounded. German truck drivers often refused to complete their deliveries, even when offered incentives for working overtime. German drivers were also accustomed to having beer at lunch, a practice strictly prohibited in the United States. The parent company began to realize it needed managers who knew the country and the culture. This was an importance lesson for us.

In Italy, one especially candid official explained that in his country, extra gratuities for poorly paid customs officers were "expected, shared with the customs managers, unofficially condoned by the government, and needed for furniture at many of the customs facilities." That certainly did not fit into our plans, but for those companies "expecting rapid customs clearance," it might be a cost of doing business. We were also going to need a simplified preclearance system for small packages similar to the one designed for Canada, and that was not available in Europe.

In 1980 the European Common Market was composed of France, West Germany, Belgium, Luxembourg, the Netherlands, Italy, Great Britain, Ireland, and Denmark. Movement of goods and documents between these countries was very different from that in the United States. First, the geography is completely different: London, Amsterdam, and Paris are all within 200 miles of Belgium, and Frankfurt is only 250 miles away, making surface transportation quite an effective way of providing overnight service. Furthermore, the countries are comparable in size to many of our states, which reminded Fitz of his UPS experience in Rhode Island. When he had tried to sell overnight service there, one of his prospects had responded, "Why should I use you when I can do that with a shopping cart?"

Transport regulations, business conventions, employee practices, languages, social customs, traditions, and holidays varied by country and even within some countries. Most of the European postal services were government-owned monopolies that were not inclined to give up any part of their turf. Shipments between countries involved customs inspection, duties, and endless paperwork. It was becoming clear that we would have to rely on European nationals to set up and manage most of the local operations, just as we were doing in Canada.

I eventually concluded that there was not a significant market for overnight priority air service between most of the industrialized Western European countries, nor was there a need for our service within the countries of the Common Market, so I began to focus primarily on transatlantic service.

THE ADVANCED PROJECTS GROUP

Back in Memphis, other changes were afoot. Between fall 1980 and early 1981, new executive managers replaced most of the senior vice presidents. Pete became the president and chief operating officer. In September, Art was elevated to the position of vice chairman and assigned to head the Advanced Projects Group. Tucker, Fitz, Wes Terry, and I became part of his team.

The Advanced Project Group opened new offices 10 miles from the corporate offices in Memphis, ostensibly to allow us to concentrate on our new assignments. We saw the move as an opportunity for the veterans who had birthed the company to provide for its future development. However, some viewed the relocation as a means to keep us from interfering with the day-to-day operations. Others saw it as a change to a more structured approach to management. Irrespective of his reasons, Fred now wanted to change his relationship with the original senior executives and made a conscious effort to separate us from the rest of the organization.

The former senior executives began to drift away, each with his own reasons. Charles had resigned at the beginning of 1980 and became a consultant to the company on technical matters. Tuck resigned the following February, shortly after hiring his replacement to head the Legal Department. Vince resigned to return to his consulting background and helped to develop marketing plans for new services.

THE ZAPMAIL BUSINESS CENTER PROJECT

Fred now began to alter his view of Federal Express, envisioning the company as a business communications entity. In June 1981 the company introduced the *Overnight Letter*, a document-sized envelope holding up to two ounces, for a flat fee of $9.50. Fred next reasoned that by converting the Customer Convenience Centers to Business Centers and installing the latest high-speed facsimile machines, Federal Express could offer a nationwide same-day document delivery service. At that time, transmission rates were slow, fax machines were not compatible between different manufacturers, the copy quality was poor, and the equipment was expensive. Fred authorized an all-out commitment to develop ZapMail, a plain-paper electronic document transmission service offering door-to-door delivery of high-quality fax documents in less than two hours.

Wes Terry, the only member of the Advanced Project Group involved in the ZapMail Business Center project, began investigating potential acquisitions of office supply companies and national convenience printers. While Art worked with Fred to look for air transportation alternatives, including the use of dirigibles for heavy domestic movements and the Concorde for transatlantic service, we filed an application for scheduled all-cargo authority from Memphis, Boston, and New York to Western Europe.

As part of my international market review, I accompanied the ZapMail project team to Japan to meet with manufacturers of advanced facsimile machines. The Japanese models used digital transmission techniques, took less than one minute per page, had better scanning resolution, and were designed to be compatible with other manufacturers. The ZapMail project team needed to move quickly, before technology advances did away with the need for our projected service.

END OF THE ROAD

In June 1981, I wrote a memo for Fred, summarizing my regular reports and ending with the following paragraph:

> Frankly, there is little more that I can or should do without action from you and our Board of Directors. . . . We have come about as far as we should without further clear and direct authorization from you.

In recognition of the current situation, further activity on my part should be suspended until you have reached a decision and made a public pronouncement concerning our intentions relating to International Operations.

One positive thing to come out of all this work was Fred's suggestion that we change the brand name to FDX or FedEx for the international market. I too felt that such a name would be more in keeping with the international flavor we observed in Europe and would eliminate the assumption that we were somehow part of the U.S. federal government. The FedEx designation wasn't adopted until 1994. At our meeting, Fred and I jointly decided that I would relocate to the East Coast, open an office in Washington, D.C., and begin assembling a staff to finalize plans for operations to Western Europe. I was elated to get a green light for the next phase.

The Canadian authorities had approved our application to fly directly into Montreal and Toronto beginning in May 1981, and responsibility for coordinating the expansion of our Canadian operations was added to my list. Cansica became our licensee for all inbound and outbound ground operations in Canada and helped me to experience firsthand the unique requirements of operating an international service.

I moved to Maryland in August with Linda, my new bride and former associate at Federal Express. The properties group located office space in Washington, D.C., that I thought was too large but that Fred justified by noting that our lobbyists and visitors from the corporate staff could share the facility with the international planning group. As furniture and office files began to arrive, I learned that the Washington contingent of the international planning group would consist of one person—me. I became the exile sharing the office with lobbyists and corporate visitors.

During the end of the year and the first half of 1982, I maintained a busy schedule, studying European competitors, meeting with customs officials, seeking information from airport managers, and contacting airlines offering to assist us with our transatlantic service. However, my efforts were second in importance to the ZapMail project. Convinced that he had stumbled across a huge technological breakthrough, Fred committed all our available resources to ZapMail. International expansion could take what fell off the table. I was becoming disillusioned once again.

By the latter part of 1982, support for the transatlantic service was almost nonexistent. Fred wanted to use the Concorde SST for the air link, but he did not want to begin the service until the international transmission network for ZapMail was operational. Westbound, the Concorde could provide overnight service from the United Kingdom to the United States, but eastbound service would be no better than second-day. Service from and to the European continent added another day to the delivery schedule. The Marketing Department commissioned several extensive studies that cast considerable doubt on our ability to capture a large share of the market for this grade of service. (Courier companies were already providing comparables.)

Incorporating the Concorde into the transatlantic service was an interesting marketing concept, but in the end, questions about reliability, the high operating cost, politics, and European national pride doomed the effort.

My substitute version for the transatlantic service envisioned our own aircraft between Memphis and London, with feeder aircraft to some Common Market destinations and local licensees for each country—similar to the Canadian operation. I pressed for a final decision on the plan. However, no approval would be granted until the ZapMail network was complete.

Meanwhile, activity at the Memphis offices of the Advanced Projects Group was winding down. Tucker left the company at the beginning of the year. Art formally announced his resignation in March. Wes Terry, whose search for acquisitions was on hold because of delays in the ZapMail program, decided to leave the company. Fitz, monitoring the delivery and performance of the new-style diesel vans, was bored with his mundane role and yearned for the exciting challenges of the earlier days. "It was just a place to go hang out," he recalled. He resigned from Federal Express in June. Mike was nearing the end of his entrepreneurial excursion; distressed from the rigors of the Superhub and frustrated with the growing bureaucracy, he left for a three-month sabbatical and then resigned from the company upon his return in September.

In a final effort to gain approval, I readied a presentation for Fred, hopeful of moving forward to the final phase of the project. Then came discouraging news: The ZapMail service would not be operational for at least 18 months. In fact, domestic ZapMail service did not begin until July 1984, and regular transatlantic service did not commence until June 1985.

Fred and I had our last meeting in October 1982, when we agreed that I would resign effective the end of the year, after turning my international planning files over to the company. It was a disappointing ending to a decade-long series of exciting events and rewarding experiences. It was an unpleasant end to a memorable part of my life, a parting without closure.

Only Fred, Jim Riedmeyer, and Pete Willmott remained of the original senior management group. Pete remained for another four months before resigning. Jim resigned a few years later.

A NATURAL TRANSITION

A few of the senior management group who were key contributors to the early and ongoing success of the company, including Art Bass, Vince Fagan, and Jim Riedmeyer have completed their journey of this lifetime. The ones who remain have actively participated in developing the content of this book. In the following paragraphs, they offer their thoughts, perspectives, and personal recollections about the company:

Art Bass (from previously published documents): I am not sure of the ingredients that made a good cake, but the one that fell off the shelf was a good one. This assemblage of creative talent at the outset is what distinguished Federal Express from many contemporary companies. With sheer courage and audacity, Fred pulled off a miracle. We were all privileged to share that experience.

Mike Fitzgerald: We had the opportunity to start something from the ground up and the freedom to infuse the things identified as the best around—the techniques and the ways to treat people. We faced crises that would have over-whelmed others and found that we could handle them, and if the things we implemented were not working out, we were able to change on the fly. If the best recruiters in the country were tasked with assembling a group that was as bright, as compatible, and as collegial as the original management group, they could not do it. We were friends and, when necessary, could subjugate our own outlook and gain important knowledge from others.

Creation of the division structure was not a wise move on our part. In the end, there was not an orderly transition of the senior officer group. We left too suddenly and without preparing our replacements. It was not good for us and it was not good for the company.

Tuck Morse: Federal Express was a great place to work. It was a constant soap opera; a cliff-hanger of major propor-tions. Fred dumped his entire inheritance into the company and was full speed ahead without concern for his personal finances. I originally assumed that the camaraderie and the cooperative atmosphere were a normal occurrence in a com-pany. Now I know that was the unique essence of Federal Express.

It was a rewarding if sometimes turbulent experience. I look back on it fondly. After we completed the financing, politics and bureaucracies started developing, and I spent most of my time nonproductively, arguing with others about some miniscule problem. I saw people who had not been through the fire spending all of the money that we had come by with some difficulty, and it just turned my stomach. It was not right for me any longer.

Ted Weise: FedEx was a learning and application of knowl-edge experience that few people ever have a chance to expe-rience. There was a complete dedication and commitment to the company and to Fred, at least during the first five or six years. I recall the innocence of Fred and all of us, not realizing the difficulties that lay ahead. Working with such talented people to help build a completely new service industry was extraordinarily satisfying. There were contentious times of course, some manufactured, some just due to the enormous growth. When I talk to executives who have been involved since the early days of their companies, they are amazed by the continuing energy and dedication of the FedEx employees compared to their organizations. [Ted stayed with FedEx for 26 years and became president of the operating company.]

Peter Willmott: Federal Express was a fabulous experience, easily the best business experience I ever had or ever will have. It was high risk, high reward. It was tough—we all worked like mad—but it was worthwhile and we all got a lot of satisfaction out of participating in the creation of a new business. It has absolutely changed the way people do business in the world.

Furthermore, how many times do you see a person who has the idea finance the idea, become the CEO of the new venture, work to change the regulations governing the company, and then still lead it when it is a very large mature company? That is the classic thing that people say can't be done. Fred is just remarkable.

Expanding on Willmott's views, I believe that Fred operated from a personal code that may have been different from my own, but I never had occasion to doubt his sincerity in wanting the best for the company, its nonexecutive employees, and its shareholders. He obviously enjoyed the power and status that come with running a large corporation, but unlike many other chief executives, he has not used that position for personal gain.

Each of us from the original management group had difficult moments with Fred, but the positive experiences far outweigh the troublesome incidents. He was and is an incredible leader, but ours was strictly a business relationship. He used the senior management group to reach his goal and then discarded its members, but that is just the way he operated. Looking back, I can see the platoon leader mentality according to which he protected the senior management group without befriending individuals. Fred was our respected leader and a critical part of the senior management group, but when the time came to exercise his executive powers for what he believed to be the good of the company, he did not hesitate to ignore our past relationships.

We stayed as long as we did because we liked the challenges and were happy creating the wonderful adventure. We all continue to have the greatest respect for Fred—the risks he took, the leadership he exercised, and his ability to motivate the entire group.

Most new companies go through natural stages of development as they grow and prosper. Ownership and decision making in the startup stage generally rest in the hands of one or a few founders who also supply the funds. This stage for Federal Express occurred when Fred worked out the details of his concept, hired the consultants to identify the market for the service, and assembled a small team that started the initial operations. The structure was informal, operations were developed on the fly, and entrepreneurial spirit was king.

After Federal became profitable, the company entered the next stage of development, commonly referred to as the survival or viability stage. During that stage the company generated enough free cash to operate and grow without outside funds. We tended to move toward a more structured organization and to use more analytical approaches to evaluate new opportunities. Management changed from an entrepreneurial to a more cautious, centralized focus as Fred began to exercise complete control of the company.

The management team that guided the company through the first two stages created its cultural DNA and set the pattern for success. When the group was shunted aside and assigned to relatively mundane tasks, it was troubling to watch the newcomers carve out their turf with little thought of the early struggles. However, companies transitioning from startup to corporate giant have to face this issue. The skills and personalities that make startups successful are seldom what is needed to manage large multinational enterprises. Change is natural and, ultimately, we must all pass the torch.

Fred may have seen the need for a new management team, one that accepted his directives without question. That was not a role for the initial senior executives. Fred gave the original senior officers an easy out by establishing the Advanced Projects Group. Corporations in similar stages of development frequently replace their original executives with professional corporate managers. Fred chose to place his mentors in positions from which they would seek new opportunities outside the company—that was his way of making the transition.

On the other hand, Fred has defied the conventional wisdom that contends founders normally do not have the necessary skills to manage larger, more mature organizations. During the next phase of growth, bureaucracy, hierarchical reporting relationships and tight operational control reigned supreme. During this third stage, Fred and his new team of senior executives were able to build on the foundation established during the first decade and lead the company to new levels of success. The original senior executives would have had difficulties contending with the multi-layered structure of the third stage. Fred, in contrast, seemed to thrive in this environment. He is unique.

LOOKING BACK

Federal Express has succeeded in ways most of us could not imagine as we struggled through the early years. The original hub-and-spokes concept was sound, Fred's leadership was solid, and the original senior management group added practical operational experience, technical expertise, and marketing skill to the equation. This team built an environment in which creativity, inspiration, motivation, and innovation could thrive, and encouraged expansive thinking that generated new ideas, new processes, and new concepts.

The company, through the devoted and never-say-die attitudes of its people, persevered to overcome seemingly insurmountable obstacles. FedEx benefited from informed decisions initiated by management and from the enthusiastic responses of operating personnel and independent supporters. However, several situations might have produced a different outcome, as the following examples illustrate:

- If the Federal Reserve had accepted Fred's proposal, what would have become of the concept for Federal Express?

- What would have happened if United Parcel had agreed to provide pickup and delivery service for Federal Express?

- What would have happened if Colonel Crown had not convinced General Dynamics to provide interim financing?

- If the local banks had grounded the fleet, what would have happened to the company?

- What would have happened if Pan Am had carried out its threat to sell the remaining Falcons?

- If Commercial Credit had foreclosed on its loan, what would have happened to FedEx?

- What would have happened to the company if Emery or UPS had started competing operations immediately?

- If the U.S. Postal Service had successfully invoked its monopoly status, what would have happened to Federal Express's lucrative Courier Pak and Overnight Letter business?

- If the original fuel allocation had not been increased during the Arab Oil Embargo, what would have happened?

- What would have happened if Charlie Lea, New Court, and the Rothschilds had not become interested in Federal Express?

- If Fred and the defiant senior management group had departed, what would have happened to the company?

- What would have happened if the large national banks had foreclosed on their loans?

- If Congress had not passed the bills deregulating the airline industry, what would have happened to Federal Express?

Looking at all of the potential problems, one may easily conclude that a large amount of good fortune affected the outcome of our efforts. In truth, most of the crises were skillfully managed without damage to the organization. Determination and quick thinking allowed us to rise above unexpected roadblocks and solve the dilemmas we had naïvely created.

Other outcomes may be postulated, but in each of the above cases, dedicated people would have found alternative ways to achieve success. What counts here is the determination and foresight to rise above the difficulties. Everything that made the company successful happened for a reason—our determined staff refused, time and again, to accept defeat.

Fred's stubborn optimism and tenacious determination, coupled with the skill and legal proficiency of Nat Breed and Tuck Morse, allowed the company to overcome the regulatory and legislative roadblocks. Aided by the talent and commitment of Charlie Lea, Brick Meers, and their associates, Fred's unceasing quest for financial assistance ultimately provided the funds to develop the entire nationwide network. The founding principles and culture that stressed the importance of truthful communications, job security, equality, openness, advancement opportunity, and training developed a self-reliant workforce composed of dedicated, die-hard employees. These very special people, in whose veins runs the company's "purple blood," are the real heroes of the FedEx story. They were in the early years, and continue to be, the heart and soul of the business.

The strength of FedEx originated with Fred's imaginative concept and charismatic leadership, coupled with the dynamic operating team, Vince Fagan's marketing strategies, the technical genius of people like Charles Brandon, and most of all, the enthusiastic *people* like those represented in this book. Most of the people who helped to build Federal Express during the turbulent early years have gone on to other successful careers.

Each of us creates the kind of life he or she leads and the events within that life. For me and for those who were there with me, building Federal Express from concept to triumph was a wonderfully rewarding business adventure. It was a once-in-a-lifetime opportunity, and I am pleased to have been a part of FedEx's incredible journey to success. It was an enjoyable experience, a gratifying experience, and, to say the least, an exciting experience. I loved the camaraderie, and I am pleased to have shared those times with my friends and the people of Federal Express.

As most of the original senior managers were leaving or planning to leave Federal Express, there was widespread concern that our departures would create a void in the organization. Vince, however, assessing the relative strength of the company, made the following observation:

> This management group and the people who have supported our leadership have created such a head of steam that nothing can kill Federal Express in the next 10 years. No matter what occurs, the momentum we have created will carry this organization through the next decade. After the next decade, new competitors will copy our operating systems and begin catching up from a systems and technology standpoint. Beyond that, the company will succeed or fail based upon the decisions made by our replacements.

PART VI

A New Model for Success

30

People Are the Wind beneath Our Wings

Federal Express was not just a good idea—it was and still is about dedicated people. The company was conceived and guided by Fred Smith, nurtured by an entrepreneurial management team that established its form and structure, and nursed into being by dedicated employees. All of us struggled to help the company grow. We nudged it along with love, enthusiasm, passion, excitement, and strength of will. During the formative years, the organization was fortunate to have an exceptional management team—but the real force behind Federal's success then and now is the passionate, tireless, resourceful, innovative, motivated, and never-say-die employees who support the managers.

As we struggled through the early stages, our employees unselfishly shared their creative abilities, maintained a mutual respect for other team members, and developed a focus aimed at collectively achieving the company goals. These individuals remained loyal to the company through all the difficulties and turmoil of the startup.

To quote Fred Smith from the 1983 annual report, Federal Express was founded with "every employee and every piece of equipment devoted to solving customers' problems by providing reliable, on-time service. The realization that they are truly needed, and that they share in this dependence, is a powerful force motivating all employees . . . who *are* Federal Express to the customer."

Fred continued to stress the human element in 1989: "The Federal Express network is far more than information systems, airplanes and delivery vans. By far its most important component is the human one, the Federal Express employees whose ongoing efforts account for our continuing prosperity. The network may well be the product, but people remain the lynchpin."

In the field of human resources, Federal Express has developed a praiseworthy approach to business based on the ethical elements of its lodestar mantra—*people, service, profits.*

FedEx begins with a detailed and careful selection process for new employees, followed by a formal indoctrination program. Equitable wages and salaries are provided, and a complete benefits program covers the standard elements of holidays, vacations, sick leave, health insurance, pension programs, funeral leave, and maternity benefits. The company goes beyond the standard package to provide disability benefits, flexible personal leave, special bonuses, profit sharing, employee stock ownership programs, and a tuition refund program. This chapter summarizes the other people-oriented programs and the culture that supported the Federal Express employees during the early years and continue to this day.

OPEN COMMUNICATIONS

The first year-end gathering held in the Little Rock hangar to lay out the principles of people, service, profit evolved into an annual briefing for employees and their spouses or guests. Long before Federal Express had the luxury of sophisticated broadcast communications, we instituted annual *Employee Family Briefings* so that the spouses of our employees could share in the excitement of the company. The sessions, each conducted by an officer of the company in Memphis and in other operating areas, were structured to acquaint everyone with the events of the past year and to share plans for the upcoming year. They were an open forum for the audience to ask questions about activities at the company and a means for recognizing those who every day responded to the challenge of building the company.

Memphis managers and executives domiciled in Memphis, when visiting other cities, typically rode the Falcon jump seat. The trip began with a midnight visit to the hub for discussions with the sorting teams. Brief discussions with the flight crews as they checked en route weather and filed their flight plans preceded the boarding of the aircraft. The small jump seat wedged between the two pilots was far from comfortable but was always a stimulating experience and an excellent opportunity to exchange information about company operations with the flight crew.

Each company facility received a daily report that contained the system's overnight package volume and the previous day's service level. We also issued company-wide reports of possible aircraft delays, along with other general information such as new city additions, pending regulatory changes, and job openings. This information, posted along with corresponding local data, continually focused attention on our two key operating indices and provided expanded information for our managers' daily "morning briefing" with facility operating personnel. Communications that kept our associates constantly and truthfully informed about the status of the organization helped to eliminate rumors that might have been damaging during our times of crisis.

EMPOWERMENT

Empowered employees are comfortable doing the very best for their customers. Senior management does well to define the values of the company, instill that value system in the company's culture, restrict the number of strictly bureaucratic regulations, and allow people to operate without tying their hands behind their backs.

A story related by Mike Basch about empowerment at Federal Express demonstrates the point:

> Diane, one of our customer service agents, got a call from a tearful woman who explained, "You were supposed to deliver my wedding dress by noon today. It's not here and I'm getting married tomorrow. Can you help me?" Diane took the information and proceeded to call each station until finally locating the package in Detroit, over 300 miles away.

Already infused with the *purple blood* can-do spirit of
Federal Express, Diane was determined to get the package
delivered that afternoon; she chartered a small plane to
fly the package to its proper destination.

Diane did not need authorization from a supervisor or a
manager; she was empowered to make the system work for the
customer.

OUR OPEN-DOOR POLICY

Federal Express maintains an open-door policy throughout the
company whereby employees at every level can comfortably discuss problems or suggest changes with their own supervisor or
anyone in management. Federal Express's open-door policy is not
just a meaningless slogan; it is a manifestation of everything critical to the success of the venture. The open-door policy encourages associates to offer suggestions for improving operations
or for modifying unnecessary or ill-conceived policies and procedures. One of the most frustrating experiences for an employee
is to follow policies that to him or her are unreasonable or just
plain ridiculous.

On one occasion, I received a call from the accounting department notifying me that my division financial analyst had rented
a full-size car for one of his trips. The clerk explained that our
policy required a compact rental car on business trips whenever
possible. I responded, "Well, Henry's own car is a Lincoln, so I
am sure that he considers the Ford to be a compact model. Why
are we even spending time on such a trivial matter? Perhaps
we should change this policy," I offered. The clerk agreed, but
reminded me that the policy had my signature at the bottom. The
rigid policy became a guideline.

On another occasion, Fred received a note from one of the
Phoenix couriers requesting air conditioning in the vans. It seemed
to most of us a reasonable request, but Dennis, noting that UPS
did not have air conditioning, responded, "I don't think they need
it." Fred thought about it for a while, concurred that it sounded
like a reasonable request, and said, "Dennis, I want you on an air-

plane to Phoenix Sunday night to ride in the vans for a whole week. If you come back to this meeting and tell me that we don't need air conditioning there, we won't get it." Dennis called him on Thursday. "Fred," he said, "I had a thermometer with me yesterday; it was 116 degrees in the cab of that van, and dry heat or not, that is hot. Let's air-condition the vans."

From the beginning, Federal Express has invited and acted on employee and customer communications and assessments, and acknowledged outstanding employee performance with appropriate recognition and rewards. The continuing response to suggestions or complaints from employees encourages meaningful communications throughout the company. By listening to employees, management is better able to understand their concerns and to develop appropriate responses to their needs. Just as customers can help to define the elements of a business, ideas from employees can help to formulate meaningful personnel policies and practices. Management *must* allow employees to question and challenge inappropriate policies and directives. By keeping an open-door attitude, managers continue to learn from those on the front line who are required to follow company directives.

COOPERATIVE RELATIONSHIPS

Everyone involved in creating the organization and operating scenarios needs to have access to a wide range of meaningful information and must be comfortable enough to use that information for the company good. In other words, it is necessary to eliminate the bureaucratic silos and empower the people. Executives need to make certain that operating people stay connected to the fundamental identity of the organization. Who are we? Who do we aspire to become? How will we get there? Where are we now? People need to be able to reach past traditional boundaries and develop *relationships* with others anywhere in the system, to have the flexibility to assist one another whenever and wherever the need arises, and to take independent action in order to keep the system functioning.

If a courier is running late or has an unusually heavy load and risks missing delivery commitments, for example, other couriers share the load and help to make the deliveries. Department heads are encouraged to offer their assistance to others who need help on lagging projects. Field managers who develop new and effective ways to operate their stations share their concepts with others. This has evolved into a program called *Best Demonstrated Practices* —sharing proven improvements with the entire company. In short, everyone is encouraged to work in an open, cooperative environment, urged to use her or his creative talents, permitted to cross departmental boundaries, and supported in her or his effort to improve the level of customer service.

COMMUNICATING INTENT WITH BUDGETS

Budgeting—the mere word causes anxiety for even the bravest operating managers—is really another form of communication within an organization. The way Federal Express began the process was simple enough: The marketing department identified new cities for the network, provided the timing of the additions, and developed a monthly forecast of the package volumes. Next, we added special or new programs planned for the year and published the results to all parts of the company. Each operating department then analyzed the effect of the upcoming changes, calculated departmental needs, and submitted the projected cost for the upcoming year. The process, which involved all supervisors, managers, and executives, communicated intent, provided a roadmap for the year, and established a baseline for predicting performance.

EMPLOYEES EVALUATE MANAGEMENT

Early in our development, we initiated the *Survey Feedback Action Program* (SFA), a voluntary, anonymous annual survey in which employees evaluate company practices and policies, as well as rate their immediate supervisor. Program administrators hold feedback sessions with employees to present the results of the survey and to discuss measures to address employee concerns. In addition, SFA scores affect the manager's compensation and qualification for advancement. This concept is not unique to Federal

Express, but its application and follow-up are so complete that employees have a high level of confidence in the program. If the program is properly conducted, employees look forward to participating, knowing that their opinions count and that, based on their input, the company will take remedial measures.

SECURITY FOR EMPLOYEES

From its inception, Federal Express made a commitment to reasonable employment security. The company has always gone to extremes to retain employees despite financial constrictions, program or business cancellations, and economic downturns. During times of great stress, we redistributed work assignments in order to avoid employee layoffs, much as we did by temporarily using our excess pilots as salesmen and station managers. When FedEx discontinued the ZapMail program, all of the people involved in that project were reassigned to other duties in the company. FedEx continues to value its employees and follows its commitment to avoid layoffs except when the future of the company is in jeopardy.

HIRING FROM WITHIN

Another commitment to employees is the promise to hire from within whenever possible. An expansive training program enables employees to continually upgrade their knowledge and skills in preparation for future opportunities within the company. All job openings are posted, and associates can bid for any opening so long as they meet the job requirements. Persistently hiring from within an organization builds trust: Employees know they have the opportunity for advancement or career change without leaving the company.

GUARANTEED FAIR TREATMENT

We further enhanced employee security by instituting the *Guaranteed Fair Treatment Program*. Any employee unable to resolve a dispute with a manager or supervisor has the absolute right to file a complaint that commences a review by other management and executive personnel. In the first review, three other senior managers—one selected by the employee, one selected by the manager, and one appointed independently—examines the circumstances of the complaint and renders a decision. That decision, if unsatisfactory to either party, may be appealed to a second review board composed of vice presidents selected in the same manner as those involved in the first review. If the parties are still not satisfied with the outcome, a third assembly composed of senior executive officers renders a final decision. This three-step process has been a consistent morale builder for all employees at Federal Express. It ensures redress for injustices or mistakes made by management.

MAINTAINING A FAVORABLE IMAGE

We always highlighted the exceptional quality of our employees and wanted to convey an image of professionalism through them. When we provided airline-like uniforms, shippers began to view our employees in an entirely different light; they became welcome visitors even to plush corporate offices. Those uniforms helped to distinguish us from our competitors. However, long pants were uncomfortable in warm weather, ties got in the way, and we needed to standardize the jackets for cold climates. Something more comfortable and practical was needed, so we set up an employee committee to design new uniforms. Empowered employees were able to meet our requirements while satisfying their own.

Creating uniforms for our flight crews was another challenge. In the beginning, the leather flight jackets stressed our hard-driving competitive nature. As we acquired new facilities and our flight crews expanded, however, pilots wanted to shed that image and look like commercial pilots, especially as they walked through airports and strolled through hotel lobbies. New uniforms designed with strong input from the crews soon helped to create the image that said our pilots were part of the commercial aviation community. Self-image is important to everyone, and pilots are no exception. Once again by listening to our employees, we created a favorable image for them and for the company.

GOLDEN FALCON AWARDS

Federal Express has always acknowledged employees that take special actions to meet or exceed customer service expectations. The company now formally recognizes outstanding employee actions through its Golden Falcon awards. Melody Harrison, a courier in Jackson, Mississippi, received the award, for example, for tracking down the location and condition of a fellow courier injured in an accident, then driving 40 miles to the site of the damaged vehicle. After spending an hour prying open the door of the van, she made certain that the packages made it to the Memphis hub. Mark Horton, a courier based in Oklahoma City, received the award for delivering his packages with a borrowed bicycle when his van would not start.

Others who have received this recognition include a courier who saved the life of a stranger trapped in a wrecked car, a courier who drove over 200 miles out of her way on Christmas Eve to deliver medicine to a sick child, and an employee who walked 15 miles to work with ice and snow on the ground when his regular ride fell through. At Federal Express it's all about people committed to service and a company that values its employees and customers.

A DIFFERENT KIND OF CORPORATE CULTURE

FedEx's commitment to security for employees, its open and honest dealings with customers, its dedication to innovative service improvement programs, and its ongoing efforts to improve long-term financial benefits for its investors are approaches worthy of emulation for any business.

By valuing its employees, customers, and investors, FedEx sets a standard for performance excellence and validates the ethical approach to business. Throughout the organization there exists a condition of true equality—regardless of job title, skin pigmentation, or gender—that encourages personal responsibility and creates unity of purpose. FedEx continues to be true to the ethical values of its founding.

FedEx reaffirmed these values in 2004, when the company purchased Kinko's. The marketing department had this to say about the new logo incorporating the FedEx colors:

> The colorful icon represents the collection of three kinds of FedEx services available at these locations—orange for the FedEx time-definite global express shipping services, green for the day-definite ground shipping services, and blue for the new retail business service centers. At the heart of the icon, where the three colors converge, is *purple*, which symbolizes the can-do spirit shared by all FedEx companies.

FedEx values its people, and they, in turn, are still the "wind beneath the wings" of the company's success.

31

Changing How the World Does Business

The most significant achievements of FedEx since 1982 are linked to the evolution of our global culture and the purchase of companies that widened the scope of operations.

The company's second decade, ending in 1992, was a time for unfettered expansion as gross revenue climbed to nearly seventeen times that of the first decade. The company extended its reach to 90 percent of the Canadian population; all of Puerto Rico; Mexico; more than twenty Caribbean islands; and much of South America. European operations covered London, Paris, Frankfurt, Milan, Brussels, Geneva, Zurich, Basel, Antwerp, Amsterdam, Eindhoven, and many smaller communities. After the purchase of Flying Tigers in 1989, direct Asian service included Tokyo, Osaka, Hong Kong, Taipei, Singapore, Seoul, and Panang. By the end of 1992, the company fleet had grown to 444 planes, including 151 B-727s, 45 wide-bodies, and 248 feeder aircraft; employees numbered just over 84,000.

The third decade witnessed continued expansion of the company, both geographically and in its service offerings. In the middle of the decade, the company entered the small-package ground delivery industry and the less-than-truckload freight market when it purchased Caliber Systems, Inc. In 2000 the company officially changed its name to FedEx Corporation, the name most familiar to its customers worldwide.

During the third decade, FedEx management built on the base created in the first two decades, moving the company to the forefront of respected international service organizations. In addition to offering time-definite express service worldwide, the corporation included a small-package ground service division, a freight division, exclusive-use nonstop door-to-door delivery service, customs brokerage, and supply chain services. The systems and innovations pioneered by FedEx have truly changed how the world does business.

ENHANCED INVENTORY MANAGEMENT

Historically, manufacturers maintained large inventories of components needed to build their products and shipped finished goods from production facilities to numerous storage warehouses, located in high-cost areas near consuming markets, in anticipation of demand. Some markets experienced excess demand and product shortages, while other areas suffered from lower-than-expected demand and excess inventory. These conditions led to disappointed customers, produced excess handling and storage charges, created high inventory carrying costs, and eventually resulted in the sale of some goods at distressed prices or destruction of obsolete inventory.

Today, in part because of FedEx, manufacturers can maintain reduced inventories of production components because items in short supply can be replaced overnight on an emergency basis. Furthermore, finished goods can be shipped directly to retail sales outlets on an as-needed basis, or even from factory to consumer, greatly simplifying the chain of supply.

Production can be planned on a global basis and inventory forecasts no longer need to anticipate the vagaries of individual market conditions. Transportation costs for inventory relocations and warehousing expenses for inventory safety stocks are lowered. Write-off of excess inventory and obsolete production is minimized.

Slow-moving parts can be consolidated and stored at a single location. For example, one company that was storing slow-movers at over 160 field branches now keeps all of that inventory at one location, providing better, more responsive service to its customers and technicians. Another company stores all its slow-movers in California where a late-afternoon order can be picked up by its New Jersey service rep early the next day.

LOWER PRODUCTION AND DISTRIBUTION COSTS

With rapid, reliable, and ubiquitous transportation, production facilities can be situated in areas most conducive to economical production. FedEx can merge system components into a single delivery irrespective of disparate component shipping locations.

Today, you can order a personalized computer system and expect delivery within one or two days. The desktop unit can be built and shipped from one location, the keyboard from another facility, the printer from a third area, and the software from a fourth location—and all delivered to the customer at the same time, anywhere in the world. FedEx provides a service that enhances reliability and reduces distribution expenses worldwide.

A European company, for example, set up a nationwide distribution network for the United States. This company, which stored inventory at eight locations in its home country, can provide comparable service to its U.S. customers with just two storage locations. The difference was the speed and reliability of the FedEx network.

FASTER TO THE MARKET

Speed to market is critical for high-value products, perishables, and high-fashion goods. The FedEx network is ideal for these producers. Pentax products from Asian factories, for example, are consolidated at the FedEx hub in the Philippines, where orders are shipped direct to retailers, cutting the replenishment cycle in half and reducing inventory expenses. Shari's Berries, a California shipper of hand-dipped strawberries, trusts the network for overnight deliveries direct to 200,000 addresses annually. Louis Vuitton uses FedEx for shipments from France to Vuitton's Memphis distribution center, where the items are delivered direct to stores across the United States.

A WIDE RANGE OF CUSTOMER SERVICES

FedEx now provides special handling for hazardous medical supplies and expedited service for organ transplants. The company also offers a send-and-return service for component-part replacement, makes hotel front-desk deliveries, and provides free packaging materials such as shipping tubes; small, medium, and large shipping boxes; and document envelopes.

Shippers and consumers may currently choose from the following menu for domestic shipments: express overnight delivery by 8:30 or 10:30 the next morning or by 3:00 the next afternoon. FedEx also offers delivery the second or third business day and on Saturdays, as well as ground service with delivery in 1 to 5 business days depending on the distance to destination. International shippers are offered time-definite deliveries based on the origin and destination country. The company has instituted same-day pickup for call-in customers, simplified paperwork, drive-up kiosks, drop boxes, customer service centers, and simplified customs clearance for international shipments. The rate structure is all-inclusive based on specified service level, weight, and delivery zone, thus eliminating the onerous and confusing ancillary charges imposed by many other shipping companies for out-of-area deliveries, document preparation, and customs clearance.

FedEx was the first shipping entity to provide expedited tracing, followed by origin and destination bar-code scans, end-to-end shipment tracking, and online shipment status information. In 1996 FedEx became the first delivery service to allow its customers to process shipments on the Internet. It was one of the first transportation companies to offer a money-back service guarantee and an online viewable electronic signature and delivery time-stamp service.

The FedEx shipment tracking system exposed those vendors with inefficient order-processing and shipping procedures, forced the invention of new techniques to reduce the time between receipt and shipment of time-sensitive orders, and eliminated many of the excuses for shipment delays.

SUPPORTING ELECTRONIC COMMERCE

E-commerce enables consumers anywhere in the world to order directly from the producer or any number of distributors, and FedEx has expanded in tandem with its rise. E-commerce provides producers, no matter their size, with access to a worldwide market and a way to satisfy each customer's individual needs. From the customer's viewpoint, e-commerce offers convenience, variety, cost savings, and anonymity. FedEx has supported the growth of e-commerce by providing fast, reliable, and time-definite delivery of these goods.

FEDERAL'S INCREDIBLE GROWTH

FedEx of today bears little resemblance to the tiny entity that struggled through startup more than 30 years ago. The company has reached a size and level of success almost unimaginable in the beginning. The little company that struggled so long and hard to get off the ground is now a global giant of legendary status. FedEx is studied as a model for success in the nation's most prestigious business schools. In recognition of its pioneering contribution to the field of aviation, the Smithsonian Institution has placed the first FedEx Falcon on permanent display at the Air and Space Museum with this comment: "The Federal Express aircraft on display was the very first of a new breed of airliner, modified specifically from its original design—for the first time in the USA—to carry packages and nothing else."

New accolades are heaped on the company as it continues to innovate and deliver outstanding service. These great achievements are the results of the unique culture established many years ago and of a corporate philosophy that empowers every level of the organization.

In the years ahead, the company will undoubtedly face new and unexpected challenges, but it will remain strong insofar as it manages to combine new approaches to the marketplace with its founding values. FedEx has given us a model for new startups and has shown the business community at large the value of courage and determination. Finally, it has taught us how a fledgling company can grow and thrive against all odds. It has been a privilege to be a part of the FedEx adventure and to tell that story here.

Appendix
Time Line for the Startup, 1971 to 1982

1971

May–June

Fred Smith invests $500,000 of his and his sisters' inheritance to launch Federal Express. He purchases two Falcons from Pan Am and takes out a $3.6 million bank loan.

July

Smith proposes to transport checks for the Federal Reserve; after strong initial interest, the proposal is turned down.

November–December

Smith contacts White, Weld and Company for help in financing. Hires A. T. Kearney and AAPG to evaluate his concept. Signs a loan guarantee of $1.15 million for option to purchase twenty-three more Falcons from Pan Am.

1972

March–April

Consultants complete studies. Smith secures bank loan to purchase eight used Falcons. Federal granted FAA operating certificate for air taxi operations.

May–June

Enterprise Company makes $2.0 million capital investment. Smith begins hiring staff to start the small-package service.

July

Federal secures $13.8 million loan covering the first ten planes. The company begins six mail runs and originates full-plane charter business.

September

Smith and Enterprise Company invest additional operating funds. Federal opens the VA pilot training school.

1973

January

Federal transfers operations to Memphis and purchases Little Rock Airmotive.

February

Smith forges Enterprise Company documents to guarantee Federal's $2.0 million loan from Union Bank. Hires White, Weld to raise funds from private investors.

March–April

System test involves ten cities and generates first-night volume of six packages. Official beginning of small-package service with twenty-five cities and 185 packages.

May

General Dynamics guarantees Chase Manhattan Bank loan of $23.7 million.

July

Smith wins $27,000 at the tables in Las Vegas. New Court Securities agrees to comanage the private placement.

October

Arab Oil Embargo; fuel allocation rules announced. Network expanded to nationwide coverage with addition of major West Coast cities.

November

First round of the private placement completed: $24.5 million in equity, $27.5 million in bank loans.

1974

March

Union Bank notifies Enterprise of overdue loan. Fred admits forging documents. Investors and lenders decide to hire a new chief executive to run Federal Express. Second round of outside financing completed. Fred and his family reduced to 19 percent voting share position.

June

Howell Estes replaces Fred as chairman and chief executive officer.

September

Senior executive staff complete. New corporate offices completed. Third round of financing completed.

1975

January

Fred indicted by grand jury for forging documents.

February

Fred threatens resignation; senior managers rebel. Estes resigns. Art replaces Fred as president; Fred becomes chairman.

March

Federal launches its first business-to-business television ads.

May

CCEC threatens to repossess its planes. First month of positive cash flow.

June

Divisional structure begins. Directors agree to preliminary steps for a public offering.

July

First profitable month.

September

Federal applies for an exemption to fly DC-9s.

December

CAB denies Federal's exemption request. Fred acquitted of charges in the Union Bank forged-documents trial.

1976

April

Fred appears before the Senate and House Aviation Subcommittees asking for liberalization of cargo regulations.

May

Federal announces first year of profitability.

June

Beginning of centralized information and customer service center.

October

Federal Express cargo liberalization bill killed in the House.

1977

March–April

New television ads feature "absolutely, positively overnight service."

May

Fiscal year's profitability double previous year's.

August–September

House and Senate work for cargo deregulation.

November

All-cargo airlines are deregulated.

1978

January

First B-727 arrives in Memphis.

February

End of the decentralized divisional structure.

March

Beginning of the Memphis Superhub design project.

April

Federal's initial public offering.

June–July

Beginning of the COSMOS system design. Start of Colorado Springs development center. Beginning of service to Canada.

November–December

Completion of the company-wide centralized Customer Service Center in Memphis.

1979

May–June

COSMOS operational.

1980

March

Planning for international service begins.

September

Pete Willmott named president as Art Bass is elevated to vice chairman. Formation of the Advanced Projects Group.

1981

May

Federal receives authority for direct flights to Canada.

June

Overnight Letter introduced.

July–August

Beginning of ZapMail business center project.

1982

Other advanced projects were put on hold in favor of ZapMail. Most of the former senior officers have left or plan to leave the company.

Index

About the Author

Roger Frock, a graduate of the University of Michigan, holds a bachelor's degree in industrial engineering and a master's degree in business administration, with advanced courses in finance. Following a tour with the U.S. Navy, he joined A. T. Kearney and Company, where he spent 12 years as a consultant to airlines, motor carriers, and railways and assisted companies in improving their distribution systems. It was here that he developed the basis for the original business plan and organizational structure of Federal Express.

In 1972 he joined the small staff of Federal Express in Little Rock, Arkansas, as general manager and head of operations. He later held the title of senior vice president responsible at various times for the field operating divisions, the Properties and Facilities Department, large aircraft introduction, tactical planning, and international operations. After leaving FedEx in 1983, he founded Business Services International, Ltd., a multidimensional international consulting group serving clients in Western Europe and the United States. He later became chairman of OSO Technologies, Inc., a California-based manufacturing company.

Mr. Frock is currently the president and CEO of Quest Management, Inc., a consulting firm specializing in supply chain management. He is also the board chairman for the Institute of Metaphysical Studies, a nonprofit educational organization. His passions include racquetball, organic gardening, and sharing with others his perspectives on maintaining a healthy lifestyle. Roger resides in Apex, North Carolina, with his wife, Linda. They have three sons and one daughter.

About Berrett-Koehler Publishers

Berrett-Koehler is an independent publisher dedicated to an ambitious mission: Creating a World that Works for All.

We believe that to truly create a better world, action is needed at all levels—individual, organizational, and societal. At the individual level, our publications help people align their lives with their values and with their aspirations for a better world. At the organizational level, our publications promote progressive leadership and management practices, socially responsible approaches to business, and humane and effective organizations. At the societal level, our publications advance social and economic justice, shared prosperity, sustainability, and new solutions to national and global issues.

A major theme of our publications is "Opening Up New Space." They challenge conventional thinking, introduce new ideas, and foster positive change. Their common quest is changing the underlying beliefs, mindsets, institutions, and structures that keep generating the same cycles of problems, no matter who our leaders are or what improvement programs we adopt.

We strive to practice what we preach—to operate our publishing company in line with the ideas in our books. At the core of our approach is *stewardship*, which we define as a deep sense of responsibility to administer the company for the benefit of all of our "stakeholder" groups: authors, customers, employees, investors, service providers, and the communities and environment around us.

We are grateful to the thousands of readers, authors, and other friends of the company who consider themselves to be part of the "BK Community." We hope that you, too, will join us in our mission.

BE CONNECTED

Visit Our Website

Go to www.bkconnection.com to read exclusive previews and excerpts of new books, find detailed information on all Berrett-Koehler titles and authors, browse subject-area libraries of books, and get special discounts.

Subscribe to Our Free E-Newsletter

Be the first to hear about new publications, special discount offers, exclusive articles, news about best sellers, and more! Get on the list for our free e-newsletter by going to www.bkconnection.com.

Participate in the Discussion

To see what others are saying about our books and post your own thoughts, check out our blogs at www.bkblogs.com.

Get Quantity Discounts

Berrett-Koehler books are available at quantity discounts for orders of ten or more copies. Please call us toll-free at (800) 929-2929 or email us at bkp.orders@aidcvt.com.

Host a Reading Group

For tips on how to form and carry on a book reading group in your workplace or community, see our website at www.bkconnection.com.

Join the BK Community

Thousands of readers of our books have become part of the "BK Community" by participating in events featuring our authors, reviewing draft manuscripts of forthcoming books, spreading the word about their favorite books, and supporting our publishing program in other ways. If you would like to join the BK Community, please contact us at bkcommunity@bkpub.com.